HUDSON TAYLOR

Yours faithfully in Christ,
J Hudson Taylor

HUDSON TAYLOR

Gospel Pioneer to China

VANCE CHRISTIE

P&R PUBLISHING

P.O. BOX 817 • PHILLIPSBURG • NEW JERSEY 08865-0817

Previously issued 1999 by Barbour Books
Reissued 2011 by P&R Publishing

Scripture quotations are from The Holy Bible, King James Version, 1611.

Italics within Scripture quotations indicate emphasis added.

Chinese characters on front cover: "Gospel / Good News"

J. Hudson Taylor portrait from M. Geraldine Guinness, *The Story of the Chinese
Inland Mission*, 3rd ed., vol. 1 (London: Morgan & Scott, 1894).

Oriental scroll © istockphoto.com/stereohype

Printed in the United States of America

Library of Congress Cataloging-in-Publication Data

Christie, Vance.
  Hudson Taylor : gospel pioneer to China / Vance Christie.
    p. cm.
  Originally published: Uhrichsville, Ohio : Barbour Pub., c1999.
  ISBN 978-1-59638-236-7 (pbk.)
  1. Taylor, James Hudson, 1832-1905. 2. Missionaries--China--Biography.
I. Title.
  BV3427.T3C48 2011
  266.0092--dc22
  [B]
                        2011012622

To my wife, Leeta,
whose sunniness and godliness
have brightened and benefited so many lives—
mine most of all

Contents

A Brush with Death

Twenty-year-old Hudson Taylor sat working intently in his boardinghouse room. He was sewing together some sheets of paper into a notebook for use in recording the lectures which he attended at the London Hospital where he was a medical student. Stitching his own notebook rather than purchasing one already bound from a stationer was just one way in which Hudson sought to live as frugally as possible.

Several weeks earlier, in September of 1852, he had come to London to further his medical training, believing the Lord would have him do that as part of his preparation for missionary service in China. Here he willingly continued to carry out the spartan lifestyle he had adopted two years earlier when God first called him to be a missionary. He believed that such economizing would better prepare him for the deprivations to be faced as a pioneer missionary in China.

Just that week Hudson had found himself in a position that he had experienced more than once in previous months: Despite his frugality, his personal funds were all but exhausted; he was eagerly looking to the Lord to supply his material need soon so that he would not literally go hungry.

Hudson truly did not mind being in such a circumstance. He thought that it provided a good opportunity to develop the strong faith in God that would be needed on the mission field. The Lord had always faithfully provided for him in the past, and he was confident that this occasion would turn out no different.

The hour was getting late, and as Hudson hastened to finish stitching the notebook, he accidentally pricked his right index finger with the needle. It was such a minor wound that he promptly forgot all about it. Little did he realize that the pinprick would nearly cost him his life!

The next morning Hudson was up early. For breakfast he ate the half loaf of brown bread that he had saved from the previous night. He put a handful of apples in his coat pockets for his lunch at the hospital. On the way home that evening he would purchase another loaf of bread to eat as supper and the next day's breakfast. Brown bread and apples washed down with nothing but water—that had been his sparse diet since coming to London.

Hudson resided in the Soho district of London. He had settled there to be near his uncle Benjamin, a brother of his mother. Uncle Benjamin lived on Church Street, just around the corner from where Hudson and one of his cousins, Tom, shared a room at a boardinghouse on Dean Street. Four miles lay between Soho and the district of Whitechapel where the London Hospital was located. Hudson traversed this distance on foot each morning and evening.

"My health is good," he wrote reassuringly to his mother in Barnsley, telling her of all the exercise he was receiving but purposely omitting the details of his meager diet. "In fact, some even say I'm getting fat!" Honesty compelled him to add,

"Although this, I believe, can only be perceived by a rather brilliant imagination."

Upon arrival at the hospital that day, Hudson was involved in dissecting a body. The dissection was particularly disagreeable and dangerous because the person had died of a fever. All those involved with the dissection worked with special care, knowing that the slightest scratch, if it became infected with the fever, could lead to death.

By midmorning Hudson began to feel extremely tired. While making noontime rounds in the surgical wards he suddenly started feeling very sick and needed to rush out. He was faint for some time, but a drink of cold water seemed to revive him and he was able to rejoin his fellow students.

He continued to feel worse and worse, however. Before the afternoon lecture on surgery was over, he found it impossible to hold his pencil and continue taking notes. By the time a second lecture was completed, his whole arm and right side were throbbing with severe pain.

"Are you all right, Hudson?" one of his fellow students queried. "You do not look at all well."

"I'm afraid not," he responded. "I'm feeling very ill."

Finding it impossible to resume work, Hudson went into the dissecting laboratory to put away his equipment. There he commented to the doctor who was overseeing the dissection, "I cannot think what has come over me." He described the symptoms he was experiencing.

The doctor stated tersely, "Why, what has happened is clear enough: you must have cut yourself in dissecting, and you know that this is a case of malignant fever."

"But I was most careful while dissecting this morning," Hudson defended himself. "I'm quite certain that I do not have a cut or scratch."

"Well, you certainly must have had one," the doctor insisted. "Here, let me examine your hands." He carefully scrutinized Hudson's hands but found nothing.

Suddenly Hudson remembered the needle poke of the previous evening. Revealing this to the doctor, he asked, "Is it possible that a prick from a needle last night could have still been unclosed this morning?"

"That was probably the cause of your trouble," the surgeon confirmed. Then he advised in a grave tone, "Now get a hansom, drive home as fast as you can, and arrange your affairs immediately. For you are a dead man!"

Hudson's first response to this stunning declaration was a feeling of sorrow that he would not be able to go to China. But that was followed immediately by the reassuring thought, "Unless I am greatly mistaken, I have work to do in China, and shall not die."

He was actually glad for the opportunity to speak with the doctor, whom he knew to be a confirmed skeptic, about his blended perspectives on the situation: "Sir, the prospect of perhaps soon being with my Master in heaven gives me great joy. But I do not think I shall die. For I am quite sure that I have work to do for God in China. And if so, however severe the struggle may be, I must be brought through it."

The surgeon was unconvinced. "That is all very well," he stated impatiently, "but you get a hansom and drive home as fast as you can. You have no time to lose, for you will soon be incapable of winding up your affairs."

As he left the hospital, Hudson smiled slightly at the idea of riding home in a cab. He had never permitted himself that luxury, and by now his finances were so depleted that he could not afford it. He would just have to walk the long distance back to his residence.

Before long, however, his strength failed him, and he realized that it was futile to attempt walking the entire distance. He paid the fare to ride two horse-drawn omnibuses and eventually reached Soho.

By the time he entered the boardinghouse he was suffering greatly. He asked the servant girl to bring him a basin of hot water and a towel to bathe his head. When she returned with them, he pleaded with her about her own spiritual condition, realizing this might be his last opportunity.

He then lanced the finger that had sustained the needle prick, hoping to let out some of the poisoned blood. The pain was excruciating, and he fainted. When he regained consciousness he found that he had been carried upstairs to his bed.

His uncle Benjamin had been summoned and was there. "I've sent for my personal physician to come and examine you," he informed Hudson.

"But medical help will be of no service to me," Hudson protested. "I do not wish to go to the expense involved."

"You've no need to worry about the expense," his uncle reassured him. "The bill will be charged to me."

The doctor arrived, learned the particulars of Hudson's sudden illness, and checked him over carefully. Then he concluded: "Well, if you have been living moderately, you may pull through. But if you have been going in for beer and that sort of thing, there is no manner of chance for you."

"If sober living is to do anything for me," Hudson thought to himself, "few could have a better chance of survival than I do. Little but bread and water has been my diet for a good while now."

"You can be assured, doctor," he stated, "that I have been living temperately. I find it helps me in my studies."

"But now," said the physician, "you must keep up your strength, for it will be a hard struggle. I want you to drink a bottle of port wine every day and to eat as many chops as you can consume."

Again Hudson smiled inwardly. Even if he desired a diet like that, he knew he did not have the means for such luxuries.

"I'll see to it that he gets whatever he needs along those lines," his uncle Benjamin interjected. In the days that followed he was true to his word and covered the cost of the fine food and drink himself.

Hudson was deeply concerned that his parents should not be informed of his serious condition. He felt assured that he was not going to die, and he did not want to cause them undue distress.

Furthermore, he knew that if they came to London and found him in this weakened condition, they would insist he return immediately with them to Barnsley so they could properly care for him there. "But if that were to happen," he thought, "I would lose the opportunity of seeing how God is going to work in my behalf, now that my money has almost come to an end."

After earnest prayer for guidance, Hudson spoke to his uncle Benjamin and cousin Tom: "Promise me that you won't write to my parents. Leave it to me to communicate with them myself once I've recovered a bit."

The two relatives looked doubtful at first, but then agreed to his request. He delayed all communication with his parents until the crisis period had passed and he was starting to recover. His family members at home knew that he had been working hard preparing for an important examination, so they were not surprised when they did not hear from him.

His illness lingered long. It was a few weeks before he regained enough strength to leave his room. At that time he learned of two men from another hospital who had contracted fever through dissection wounds at around the same time he sustained his. Both those men had since died. Hudson knew that his life had been spared in answer to prayer to work for God in China.

Christian Heritage and Conversion

Hudson Taylor's ancestors on both sides of the family were devout Yorkshire Methodists. His great-grandparents, James and Betty Taylor, hosted informal Christian meetings in their cottage when, in the early 1780s, they moved to Barnsley, a mining town which at that time had a reputation for drunkenness, licentiousness, gambling, and fierce opposition to the zealous new sect of Christians known as Methodists.

Despite the opposition, a Methodist congregation soon formed in Barnsley and James served as its first lay preacher. More than once he was accosted while preaching in the town's marketplace, being pelted with stones and refuse or being knocked down and literally dragged through the mud. On one occasion two men attacked him and rubbed into his eyes a mixture of pounded glass and mud, intending to blind him. It was three months before he was able to return to work after that attack.

James never struck back at his opponents, but continued to courageously proclaim the Christian gospel. Gradually he

began to gain respect in the community and to have a significant impact on its spiritual condition. So much so, in fact, that
when John Wesley, the founder of Methodism, came to preach
in Barnsley at the age of eighty-two, he found the townspeople
very receptive to his ministry.

Wesley recorded of the occasion in his personal journal: "Friday, June 30, 1786: I turned aside to Barnsley, formerly famous
for all manner of wickedness. They were then ready to tear any
Methodist preacher in pieces. Now not a dog wagged its tongue. I
preached near the marketplace to a very large congregation, and
I believe the truth sank into many hearts. They seemed to drink
in every word. Surely God will have a people in this place."

James and Betty's oldest son, John, along with his wife,
Mary, were active members in that same Methodist congregation throughout their adulthood. John and Mary's second son,
James, followed in the ministerial footsteps of his grandfather
after whom he was named. Late in his teens the younger James
began preaching in neglected villages in outlying areas. Church
officials concluded that he was called of God to the gospel ministry and, when he was but nineteen, added his name to the list
of Barnsley's recognized Methodist preachers.

James married Amelia Hudson, the eldest daughter of
another Methodist minister who had served for a time on the
Barnsley circuit, Benjamin Hudson. James brought his bride
home to 21 Cheapside on Barnsley's marketplace on May Day
Green. Here he had been building a successful business as an
apothecary. His shop faced out onto the marketplace while the
family's living quarters were behind and above the store.

When James and Amelia discovered that they were going
to have their first child, they solemnly consecrated the child
to the Lord in the spirit of Exodus 13. They had come to share
a deep concern over the crying spiritual needs of unevange-

lized China, so much so that they were willing to pray, "Dear God, if You should give us a son, grant that he may work for You in China."

That consecrated child, James Hudson Taylor, was born on May 21, 1832. He was named James after his father and great-grandfather. He was called by his middle name, Hudson, his mother's maiden name.

James and Amelia had three other children, a son and two daughters. William was born a year or two after Hudson, but died at age seven. Amelia was born when Hudson was three years old and Louisa when he was eight.

Hudson's own health as a child was far from robust. He was such a feeble child, in fact, that for many years his parents abandoned all thought of his serving as a missionary some day.

James and Amelia educated their children at home when they were young. Amelia gathered them in the parlor behind the apothecary shop each afternoon. There she sewed while the children read aloud to her, or she would dictate sentences for them to write. She was particular about their using proper grammar and pronunciation. James taught his children French, Latin, and arithmetic. He also took them on long Saturday afternoon walks through the countryside, teaching them all he knew about birds, butterflies, and flowers.

Hudson's parents also diligently instructed their children about spiritual matters. Besides faithfully taking the children to church services, they had family devotions twice daily, after breakfast and afternoon tea. Both Old and New Testament Scriptures were carefully explained to the children during these times and fervent prayers were offered.

As the children grew older, James gathered them in his bedroom every day where he would kneel down with them beside the four-poster bed, put his arms around them, and pray for each one. He would then dismiss them to their own rooms for a time of private Bible reading.

"Learn to love your Bible," he encouraged them. "For God cannot lie. He cannot mislead you. He cannot fail."

Christian friends from in town and out in the country frequently stopped by to visit with James and Amelia in their home. Once a quarter, Methodist ministers from all over the Barnsley circuit would gather at the Chapel on Pinfold Hill to transact business and make plans. Afterward, James often invited one and all to afternoon tea at his residence.

The Taylor children enjoyed immensely listening in on the conversations on those occasions. Hudson's sister Amelia wrote years later: "We used to love to hear them talk—those local preachers gathered round our table for high tea. Theology, sermons, politics, the Lord's work at home and abroad, all were discussed with earnestness and intelligence. It made a great impression on us as children."

The subject of foreign missions was often taken up at those gatherings. James Taylor, with his special burden for China, would exclaim:

> Why do we not send our missionaries to China? That is the country to aim at, with its teeming population, its strong, intelligent, scholarly people. We Methodists glory in Wesley's motto, 'the world is my parish,' yet none of our new workers being sent out are destined for China. It seems to be taken for granted that nothing can be done or even attempted by us there.
>
> Not until this century has a single Protestant missionary sought to take the gospel to that country. Even now the Christian hospital in Canton being run by the small band of Americans is still the only mission station in all of China. Beyond the narrow limits of that single settlement lies the whole vast empire with

its four hundred million souls, amongst whom no one is living
and preaching Christ.

Such convictions had considerable impact on Hudson Taylor
and his siblings. They came to view China as the greatest, the
most neglected, and most promising of missionary lands.

As a young boy Hudson would sometimes declare, "When
I am a man, I mean to be a missionary and go to China." His
parents would exchange glances, but said nothing to him about
the prayers they had voiced before his birth. He was never told
about those prayers until after he returned from his first seven
years of service in China.

In the fall of 1843, when Hudson was eleven, he was sent off
to school for the first time. Two years later, however, he returned
home after a dissatisfactory headmaster took over the school.
Back home, Hudson began helping his father in his workshop,
learning to prepare and package medicines.

Not long after Hudson's fifteenth birthday, one of the Barnsley banks had a vacancy for a junior clerk. James, eager for his
son to learn how to keep accounts and write business letters,
made inquiry and Hudson was hired for the position.

Unfortunately, the new job did more than educate Hudson
regarding business and accounting practices. It also increased
his knowledge of the ways of the world. The people he worked
with were materialistic and skeptical toward spiritual matters.
Hudson was introduced to profane language and worldly ways
of thinking which he had never before encountered in his shel-
tered upbringing.

His coworkers ridiculed his old-fashioned notions about
God and delighted in confusing him with arguments such as:
"Christians are hypocrites. They claim to believe their Bibles,
but they live just as they would if they never read them."

Young Hudson was at a loss how to answer such criticisms, and they left him feeling greatly troubled. He began to question his conservative Christian upbringing: "Is what I've always been taught really true or is it too narrow-minded?"

Still he could not escape a thought which his parents had repeatedly emphasized: "If there is any such Being as God, then to trust Him, to obey Him, and to be fully given up to His service must of necessity be the best and wisest course both for myself and others."

But then Hudson took a wrong turn in his thinking. He concluded that he must somehow make himself a Christian through his own upright behavior and acts of service. The harder he tried, however, the more he felt like a failure.

This led to other errant conclusions: "For some reason or other I cannot be saved. So the best thing I can do is to enjoy the pleasures of this world, for there's no hope for me beyond the grave."

Hudson stopped praying altogether and started finding church and family devotions an irksome bore. More and more he adopted the outlook of his fellow employees at the bank. If they were right then he could live any way he chose, because there was no God to punish him for sinning.

At that point, however, the very God from whom Hudson was straying worked graciously and providentially in his life by allowing him to develop an infection in his eyes which forced him to resign his position at the bank after only nine months. Through this sovereign intervention Hudson was removed from the ungodly influences which had been destroying his belief in Christian teachings.

He went back to work for his father, but now was unsettled and unhappy. His inner faith conflict caused him to be gloomy and brooding much of the time. James Taylor, who did not know about the spiritual struggle raging within his son, became irritated by his moodiness. Hudson's mother, however, was more sensitive to her son's struggles and began to pray more earnestly for his spiritual welfare.

Several months later, in June of 1849, about a month after his seventeenth birthday, Hudson had an afternoon free from responsibility and found himself looking for something to read to pass the time. He browsed through the books on the family's large bookcase in the parlor but nothing appealed to him. Then he spotted a small basket of pamphlets and searched through them until he found a gospel tract which looked interesting.

Picking it up, he thought, "There will be a story at the beginning, and a sermon or moral at the close. I will take the former and leave the latter for those who like it."

In order to avoid interruption, he went out to the small warehouse in which his father stored supplies on the back of their property. He started reading with "an utterly unconcerned state of mind" about his spiritual condition or his relationship with the Lord. He fully intended to stop reading the pamphlet the moment it became prosy.

Unbeknown to him, at that very moment his mother was kneeling in prayer, pleading with God for his salvation. Amelia Taylor had gone to visit her sister in Barton-upon-Humber, some fifty miles away, and that afternoon had found herself with little to do. After noon dinner she went to her room where she was determined to remain in prayer for Hudson's conversion until she felt certain her request had been granted.

As she earnestly prayed, Hudson read about a coal miner in Somerset who was dying of tuberculosis. Some Christians visited him and shared the gospel through a series of Scripture verses. The miner was struck by the Bible's teaching that Jesus bore our sins in His own body on the cross. When the dying man was told about Christ's cry of "It is finished!" from the cross, he comprehended its significance with regard to the complete provision that had been made for his own salvation and that day prayed to become a Christian.

Hudson's attention was arrested by a single phrase in the tract, "The finished work of Christ." "Why does the author use this expression?" he wondered. "Why not say the atoning or propitiatory work of Christ?" Immediately Jesus' declaration from the cross—"It is finished!"—came to mind.

"What was finished?" Hudson pondered further. Again the answer to his own question leaped to mind: "A full and perfect atonement and satisfaction for sin. The debt was paid by the substitute. Christ died for my sins."

"If the whole work was finished and the whole debt paid, what is there left for me to do?" was his next thought. "What has been the point of all my efforts to make myself a Christian?"

Hudson later wrote of that moment: "And with this dawned the joyful conviction, as light was flashed into my soul by the Holy Spirit, that there was nothing in the world to be done but to fall down on my knees, and accepting this Savior and His salvation, to praise Him for evermore." He immediately knelt down there in the warehouse and asked Jesus Christ to become his personal Savior.

Meanwhile an assurance came to the heart of Hudson's mother that she no longer needed to continue praying. She began to praise God for the firm conviction, which she was sure was from the Holy Spirit, that her son had been converted.

A few days later Hudson told his sister Amelia of his recent acceptance of Christ but made her promise that she would keep the matter to herself for the time being. He wanted to be the first to share the joyous news with his mother when she returned.

After several more days their mother did return, and Hudson was the first to greet her at the door, exclaiming, "Mother, I've such good news for you!"

"I know, my boy," his smiling mother responded, throwing her arms around his neck. "I've been rejoicing in your news for a fortnight!"

Surprised, Hudson queried, "Why, has Amelia broken her promise? She said she would tell no one."

"Amelia kept her promise," his mother assured him. "It was not from any human source that I learned this. I know when you were converted, and it was in answer to my prayers." She then told him of her afternoon of intercession for his salvation and of the settled assurance that had come that her request had been granted.

Some time later Hudson learned that his mother was not the only one who had been praying for his salvation. One day he picked up and opened a notebook which he thought was his own but which actually belonged to his sister Amelia. His eye landed on a single sentence: "I will pray every day for Hudson's conversion." From the date that accompanied the journal entry, Hudson knew his sister had been praying daily for his salvation for a month at the time he was converted.

3

"Then Go for Me to China"

In September of that same year, 1849, Hudson's sister, Amelia, was sent away to her Aunt Hodson's boarding school at Barton-upon-Humber. In exchange, the oldest Hodson son, John, came to Barnsley where he was apprenticed to Hudson's father in his apothecary business. (Their aunt's maiden name was Hudson; Hodson was her husband's surname.)

Hudson shared his bedroom with this cousin, who had a cheerful flippancy toward spiritual matters. This arrangement took its toll on Hudson's spiritual health, for he found it more difficult to read his Bible and pray with John in the room. After the initial joy of his conversion passed, Hudson experienced a period of spiritual deadness.

God, however, used a trio of influences just at that time to bring him out of that spiritually dry period. First, Hudson read an article in the *Wesleyan Magazine* titled "The Beauty of

Holiness." This article made devotion and righteous living once again seem irresistibly attractive to him.

About that same time Hudson's church had a special series of evangelistic meetings. The Lord's Spirit worked mightily through that four-day mission, with over one hundred people coming to faith in Christ. The commitment of many of God's people, including Hudson, was rekindled through those meetings as well.

Finally, he was given a church membership card which bore the words of Ezekiel 36:26: "A new heart also will I give you, and a new spirit will I put within you: and I will take away the stony heart out of your flesh, and I will give you an heart of flesh."

"Dear Lord," Hudson pleaded, "please take away my heart of stone and give me a heart of flesh! Help me to believe the promises of your Word! My heart longs for this perfect holiness."

God granted that fervent request and his spiritual vitality returned. That experience left Hudson, as he testified, with "a deepened sense of personal weakness and dependence on the Lord as the only Keeper as well as Savior of His people."

One Sunday some time later Hudson was unable to go to church because of a serious cold. Instead, he went alone to his room to spend a protracted time in fellowship with God. "O Lord," he repeatedly prayed, "my heart is so full of joy and love and gratitude toward You. Thank You, O God, for saving me even after I had given up all hope of being saved, even after I had lost all desire for salvation." Then he added with all earnestness, "Lord, please give me some work to do for You as an outlet for my love and gratitude toward You."

God met with Hudson in a special way on that occasion. He would later write of it:

> Well do I remember, as in unreserved consecration I put myself, my life, my friends, my all, upon the altar, the deep solemnity

that came over my soul with the assurance that my offering was accepted. The presence of God became unutterably real and blessed. I remember stretching myself on the ground and lying there silent before Him with unspeakable awe and unspeakable joy. For what service I was accepted I knew not; but a deep consciousness that I was no longer my own took possession of me, which has never since been effaced.

He was sincere in dedicating himself to the Lord's service, whatever that might prove to be, yet he continued to struggle with his own sins and shortcomings. More and more he sensed his inability to gain victory over sin in his own strength. After one such occasion of spiritual defeat, he cried out to God like never before: "O Lord, break the power of sin in my life! Give me inward victory in Christ! God, if you will do that, I pledge to go anywhere, do anything, undergo whatever suffering Christ's cause might demand and to be wholly at Your disposal."

Suddenly he was struck by the feeling that he was in the presence of God, entering a covenant with the Almighty. For a moment he wished he could withdraw his promise, but felt he could not. Something seemed to say, "Your prayer is answered; your conditions are accepted."

Then, just as suddenly and clearly, God's purpose for his life came to Hudson's mind and heart. Distinctly, as if an audible voice had spoken, he heard God's call, "Then go for Me to China." From that moment on, throughout the remainder of his life, the conviction never left him that he was divinely commissioned to serve as a missionary in China.

His parents, still exercising reserve, neither discouraged nor encouraged his newly stated intent to undertake missionary service. "Use all the means in your power," they advised him, "to develop yourself spiritually, mentally, and physically. Wait prayerfully upon the Lord and remain open to His guidance, whether that be into or away from missionary endeavor."

Hudson started exercising more out of doors in order to strengthen his body. He replaced his soft feather bed with a hard mattress and dispensed with as many other home comforts as he could in order to accustom himself to rougher living conditions which he knew he was sure to encounter in the future.

He also busied himself in various avenues of Christian service. He began teaching Sunday school. Instead of continuing to go to church twice on Sunday, as had always been his custom, he started devoting Sunday evenings to visiting in the poorer sections of Barnsley. There he distributed tracts, held cottage meetings, and visited the poor and sick.

Beginning in March 1850 a group of Christian British businessmen launched a new magazine, *The Gleaner in the Missionary Field*, which was intended to promote interest in missions overseas. Hudson's family subscribed to the magazine from its inception, and he devoured each issue.

He learned of the formation of an interdenominational missionary society in London called the Chinese Association. The association intended to employ Chinese evangelists who would work with existing mission agencies to carry the gospel to the vast interior region of China, most of which had not yet been evangelized.

Hudson inquired with the pastor of Barnsley's Congregational Church if he might borrow his copy of Walter Medhurst's book, *China: Its State and Prospects*. Medhurst was only the second Protestant missionary ever to venture to China. A printer, he went to China in 1817, where he traveled inland in disguise to distribute Christian literature.

"You certainly may borrow the book," the Congregational minister responded to Hudson's request, "but, tell me, why do you wish to read it?"

"I believe that God has called me to spend my life in missionary service in China," Hudson revealed.

"And how do you propose to go there?" the pastor asked further.

"I do not at all know," Hudson responded truthfully. "But it seems probable to me that I shall need to do as the Twelve and the seventy did in Judea—go without purse or scrip, relying on Him who has called me to supply all my need."

The old minister kindly placed his hand on Hudson's shoulder and stated, "Ah, my boy, as you grow older you will get wiser than that. Such an idea would do very well in the days when Christ Himself was on earth, but not now."

Decades later, Hudson Taylor reflected on that exchange: "I have grown older since then, but not wiser. I am more than ever convinced that if we were to take the directions of our Master and the assurances He gave to His first disciples more fully as our guide, we should find them to be just as suited to our times as to those in which they were originally given."

One point that Medhurst's book emphasized was the great potential of medical missions in China. Reading this caused Hudson to start seriously considering medical studies as an excellent mode of preparation for mission work.

Books on the Chinese language were rare and enormously expensive in that day. A Chinese grammar book cost twenty dollars (one English pound was equal to five American dollars in that day) and a dictionary seventy-five or more. Hudson could afford neither. He was given, however, a copy of the Gospel of Luke written in the Chinese Mandarin dialect.

This he studied carefully. By painstakingly comparing brief verses with their equivalent in English, he was able to discover the meaning of over six hundred Chinese characters. He compiled these into a dictionary of his own and committed them to memory.

He diligently pursued other studies as well, as he related in a letter to his sister, Amelia: "I have begun to get up at five in the morning and find it necessary to go to bed early. I must study if I mean to go to China. I am fully decided to go, and am making every preparation I can. I intend to rub up my Latin, to learn Greek and the rudiments of Hebrew, and get as much general information as possible. I need your prayers."

Language studies were not the only thing on Hudson's mind during those months. One holiday break Amelia brought home as her guest the music teacher from Aunt Hodson's school, an attractive and vivacious young lady named Marianne Vaughan.

Marianne's singing and playing of the piano seemed simply heavenly to Hudson. In addition to enjoying that recreation together, Hudson, Amelia, and Marianne were able to go horseback riding. Before the holidays ended, Hudson had fallen deeply in love with Marianne, and she seemed to reciprocate interest toward him.

Hudson tried not to dwell on the fact that Marianne seemed only politely interested in China. He knew that God had called him to China, but was uncertain whether Marianne would eventually consent to go there with him. Yet he could not bear the thought of going without her. He would just have to hope and pray that the Lord would create within her a willing heart.

In the spring of 1851, Hudson happily accepted the opportunity to become the assistant to one of the leading physicians in Hull, Dr. Robert Hardey. Hudson viewed this as an excellent first step to gaining medical knowledge that he might someday use on the mission field.

Dr. Hardey was the brother-in-law of Hudson's maternal Aunt Hannah who also lived in Hull. The good-humored, popular doctor had his office and residence at 13 Charlotte Street. There Hudson went on his nineteenth birthday to begin working and living.

In addition to his private practice, Dr. Hardey was a surgeon at the hospital and for several factories, as well as a teacher at the school of medicine in Hull. Hudson attended lectures at the medical school. He also assisted Hardey in performing surgeries, dressing wounds, and dispensing medicines at his office.

After a while the bedroom in which Hudson had been staying at Robert Hardey's residence was needed for another family member, so arrangements were made for him to move to the home of his Aunt Hannah in Kingston Square. Hannah's husband, Richard, was the brother of Dr. Hardey. Richard was a photographer while Hannah was a portrait artist. They had no children of their own, so were very willing to host their nephew.

Their home was conveniently located for Hudson, being just across the street from the medical school where he attended lectures and nearby the surgery where he assisted Dr. Hardey. Richard and Hannah had many friends in Hull. Hudson enjoyed the frequent opportunities for socializing that were afforded him in their home.

But Hudson was troubled by one factor. Shortly before leaving his parents' home in Barnsley he had conducted a careful study of the Bible's teaching on financial giving and had concluded that he should contribute at least one tenth of his income to the Lord's work. Part of the salary he received from Dr. Hardey included the cost of his room and board at Aunt Hannah's. He came to believe that he really should tithe that portion of his income as well. He knew if he did, however, that he would not have enough left over to pay all his other living expenses.

After much thought and prayer Hudson decided that he would seek out a less-expensive place to live so that he could tithe his entire income. After searching, he located an available room in a cottage just outside town in a neighborhood known as Drainside. The small house at 30 Cottingham Terrace was one of a number of cottages that lined both banks of the Cottingham Drain, a stream that ran down to the sea about half a mile away.

This location, though more distant from work and isolated from relatives, proved beneficial for Hudson in certain ways. He was able to devote more time to studying Scripture, to visiting the poor, and to carrying out evening evangelistic work. In addition to saving money on his rent, he was able to economize on his eating expenses as well.

He soon discovered that he could live on much less money than he had previously thought possible. With the money he was able to save on food and rent Hudson gave generously to help the poorer people to whom he ministered. At that time he routinely gave two-thirds of his income to various facets of the Lord's work.

All this was done willingly rather than out of a sense of obligation. He later testified of that time:

> My experience was that the less I spent on myself and the more I gave to others, the fuller of happiness and blessing did my soul become. Unspeakable joy all the day long, and every day, was my happy experience. God, even my God, was a living, bright reality; and all I had to do was joyful service.

Hudson was already serving the Lord faithfully and sacrificially. God soon brought a series of events into his life, however, that both tried and deepened his faith.

4

First Tests of Faith

For Hudson it was "a very grave matter" to contemplate going to China. He realized that there he would be far removed from all human aid and would need to depend on God alone for protection, material provision, and help of every other kind. Hudson had no doubt that the Lord was completely faithful, but he did wonder whether his own faith would fail when his only recourse was to God rather than to some human source of support.

He believed that his spiritual muscles needed to be strengthened for such an undertaking. "When I get out to China," he mused, "I shall have no claim on anyone for anything; my only claim will be on God. How important, therefore, to learn before leaving England to move man, through God, by prayer alone!"

He immediately perceived his first opportunity to put this new plan into action. Dr. Hardey, perpetually occupied with numerous concerns, had asked Hudson to remind him whenever his quarterly salary was due so that it would not be overlooked. The young medical student decided, however, not to request his salary directly. Instead, he would ask the Lord to bring the matter to his employer's mind and thus encourage Hudson by answering his dependent prayer.

As the next quarterly payday drew near, Hudson spent much time in prayer, asking God to remind Dr. Hardey of his salary. The day came, but the busy doctor made no mention of his wages. Several more days passed, and Hudson continued to pray about the matter, but still his employer remained unmindful of the tardy paycheck.

Finally the day came when Hudson had left in his possession only a single coin, a half-crown piece. He was not disturbed, however. He committed the matter to the Lord in prayer and went peacefully to sleep.

The next day, a Sunday, he attended church in the morning and, as had become his custom, spent the afternoon and evening holding gospel services in the poorer sections of Hull. Throughout the day and evening his heart was full of joy with the consciousness of God's numerous blessings.

Just after he concluded the final service about ten o'clock that night, a man who was obviously very poor approached Hudson and asked him to come and pray for his wife who was dying. Hudson readily agreed, and the two set out for the man's home.

Along the way, noting that the man spoke with an Irish accent and supposing him to be a Roman Catholic, Hudson asked, "Why did you not send for the priest?"

"I did," the man responded truthfully, "but he refused to come without a payment of eighteen pence. My family has no money even for food, so I couldn't pay him."

Hudson immediately thought of the single silver coin in his pocket. He also contemplated the fact that he had almost no food of his own back at his apartment. He had enough thin porridge left for supper that night and breakfast in the morning but nothing for dinner later on Monday. Suddenly he started feeling anxious, then irritated with the man who had come to him for help.

He actually started reproving the poor man: "It is very wrong for you to have allowed matters to get to this state. You should have sought assistance from the appropriate public official."

"I did," the man stated meekly. "But I was told to come back at eleven tomorrow morning, and I fear my wife might not live through the night."

Hudson's uneasiness increased when his escort turned down a certain street. It led into a particularly rough section of Hull's Irish district. Saloons and cheap lodging houses abounded there. So violent was the area that even policemen rarely entered it in groups of fewer than four.

He had visited that neighborhood once previously, seeking to do evangelistic work. But he had been treated roughly, and his gospel tracts had been torn to pieces. On that former occasion he received a severe warning never to return. Now, however, he continued to follow the man, believing that it was his duty to do so.

They ascended a dilapidated flight of stairs and entered a wretched dwelling. There a scene of abject poverty and woeful misery confronted Hudson. Four or five children stood around the room, their cheeks and temples sunken from gradual starvation. On a wretched pallet in one corner was the exhausted mother. Her tiny baby, only thirty-six hours old, moaned rather than cried at her side.

Hudson's heart went out to the family members. He felt an inner impulse to help relieve their distress by giving them the lone coin in his possession. But he resisted the prompting, knowing the coin was his last.

Instead, he tried to share words of comfort with the family. He was so disturbed himself at that moment, he could hardly speak. Still he forced out the words: "You must not be cast down because, though your circumstances are very distressing, there is a kind and loving Father in heaven who cares about your needs."

"You hypocrite!" his conscience screamed, "telling these unconverted people about a kind and loving heavenly Father, and not prepared yourself to trust Him without half a crown."

"If only I had two shillings and a sixpence instead of half a crown," Hudson lamented inwardly, "how gladly would I give them the two shillings and keep the sixpence for myself!"

Hudson felt nearly choked and found further attempts at verbal consolation impossible. He decided to pray instead. Prayer was a delightful occupation for him at that phase of his life, and he was never at a lack for words while engaged in it. He was sure that if he simply knelt down and began to pray, relief would come to the distraught family and to himself.

"You asked me to come and pray with your wife," he said to the husband. "Let us pray." Kneeling down, he began to recite the Lord's Prayer: "Our Father who art in heaven . . ."

The words had hardly passed his lips when his conscience smote him again: "Dare you mock God? Dare you kneel down and call Him Father with that half-crown in your pocket?"

"Such a time of conflict came upon me then," Hudson later reported, "as I have never experienced before or since. How I got through that form of prayer I know not, and whether the words uttered were connected or disconnected I cannot tell. But I arose from my knees in great distress of mind."

As he rose, the poor husband and father implored him, "You see what a terrible state we are in, sir. If you can help us, for God's sake, do!"

Immediately Christ's instruction from the Sermon on the Mount flashed into Hudson's mind: "Give to him that asketh of thee." Surrendering to the prompting of God's Spirit, he put his hand into his pocket and slowly pulled out the single silver coin.

Giving it to the poor man, he stated: "It might seem a small matter for me to relieve you, seeing that I am comparatively well off. But in parting with this coin I am giving you my all. Yet what I have been trying to tell you is indeed true—God really is a Father who can be trusted."

Instantaneously a wave of joy came flooding back into Hudson's heart. He could again freely express himself, and he felt within himself the wonderful truths that he was verbalizing outwardly.

Late that night, as he made his way through the deserted streets back to his lodging, his heart was so full that he spontaneously burst out in a hymn of praise to God. "I am so thankful for this bowl of gruel as the Lord's provision for me," he thought as he ate his late supper, "that I would not exchange it for a prince's feast."

Before retiring that evening, he knelt at his bedside and reminded God of the teaching of Proverbs: "Dear Father, Your Word promises that he who is kind to the poor lends to the Lord. Would you not allow my loan to be a long one. Otherwise I will have no dinner tomorrow." Then, being completely at peace, he had a restful night of sleep.

The next morning, while eating his final bowl of porridge for breakfast, he heard the postman's knock at the door. A moment later his landlady, Mrs. Finch, came in with a small packet for Hudson. Examining the little parcel as he took it, Hudson did not recognize the handwriting. The postmark was blurred so he could not determine from where the package had come.

When he opened the envelope he found a pair of kid gloves folded inside a sheet of blank paper. As he removed these, a gold coin—half a sovereign, worth four times the amount he had given to the poor family the previous evening—fell to the floor.

"Praise the Lord!" Hudson exclaimed as he picked it up. "Four hundred percent for twelve hours' investment; that is good interest. How glad the merchants of Hull would be if they could lend their money at such a rate!" Right then and there he determined that all his future earnings and savings would be invested in the Lord's bank, a bank that he knew could never break.

Hudson did his best to economize with this unexpected supply of ten shillings. In less than two weeks, however, his funds were again exhausted. Though he continued to pray earnestly that his quarterly salary might soon be supplied, it was obvious that Dr. Hardey had completely forgotten about it.

As the end of the week drew near, Hudson began to feel quite embarrassed. Not only did he need money for food, but Saturday evening was when his rent was due to Mrs. Finch. He knew that she could ill afford to be without it. Her husband, the captain of a ship, was away at sea, and she depended on the rental income to help make ends meet.

Should he, for her sake, speak to his employer about his overdue salary? But if he were to do that, he would consider himself a failure at depending on God alone to move men in his behalf, and thus unfit for missionary service in China. Thursday and Friday, Hudson spent much time wrestling with God in prayer about these matters. He went to work on Saturday morning with a calm inner assurance that to wait on God's timing was best, and that the Lord would undertake for him in one way or another.

Late that afternoon, when Dr. Hardey had completed his rounds and had finished writing out his prescriptions, he leaned back in his office armchair and began conversing with Hudson. A committed Christian himself, Robert Hardey often discussed with his assistant, as he did on this occasion, the things of God.

Soon, with no apparent connection in thought to what he had just been talking about, the doctor paused and asked, "By the way, Taylor, is not your salary due again?"

Hudson was glad that at that moment he had his back turned to Dr. Hardey as he attentively watched over a mixture of medicine that he was boiling in a pan. At his employer's query, his heart leaped. God had surely heard his prayer and had moved the doctor to meet his need.

He had to swallow two or three times before he was able to answer. Then, keeping his eyes fixed on the pan, he responded as quietly and calmly as he could: "As a matter of fact, sir, my salary was due some little time ago."

"Oh, I am so sorry you did not remind me!" the doctor said sincerely. "You know how busy I am. I wish I had thought of it a little sooner, for only this afternoon I sent all the money I had to the bank. Otherwise I would pay you at once."

Hudson's spirit, which had begun to soar, plummeted at this unexpected disclosure. He was so stunned he did not know what to say. Fortunately, the pan of medicine started boiling over just at that moment, giving him a good excuse to rush with it out of the room. He was relieved when, a few minutes later,

Dr. Hardey left the office for his home, having not noticed his assistant's emotional distress.

As soon as the doctor was gone, Hudson fell to his knees and, for quite some time, poured out his heart to the Lord. Gradually calmness and even thankfulness and joy were restored to him. Again he felt assured that God was not going to fail him but would provide for him in some other way.

Hudson spent that evening there at the office reading the Bible and preparing the thoughts he planned to share in the various lodging houses that he would visit the next day. At about ten o'clock he put on his overcoat and began preparing to leave. He was relieved to know that Mrs. Finch would already be asleep when he arrived home. Perhaps the Lord would supply his financial needs by Monday so that he could at least pay the rent he owed by early in the week.

Just as he was about to turn out the gas lights, he heard Dr. Hardey returning to the office. The doctor was laughing heartily to himself, obviously greatly amused by something. Coming into the office, he asked for his ledger and made an entry in it.

As he did, he related to Hudson: "Strange to say, one of my richest patients just came to pay his doctor's bill. Was that not an odd thing for him to do at this unusual hour? He could have easily sent a check to cover his bill any day. But it appears that somehow or other he could not rest with this on his mind and felt constrained to come at this unusual hour to care for his obligation."

Hudson agreed that the wealthy individual's actions were indeed highly irregular, but he did not at once grasp their relevance to his current financial situation. The light dawned, however, when his employer suddenly turned and handed him some of the bank notes he had just received.

"By the way, Taylor, you might as well take these notes. I have not any change, but can give you the balance of your salary next week."

This time when the doctor left, Hudson knelt down to praise God with a heart that was overflowing with joy and thanksgiving. Far beyond merely supplying his material needs, this remarkable set of events convinced him that he might after all go as a missionary for Christ to China.

5

Further Training in London

During the summer of 1852 Hudson came to believe that the Lord would have him move to London in order to further his medical training. The previous May, the month he turned twenty, the Chinese Society changed its name to the Chinese Evangelization Society (CES) and announced in *The Gleaner* that it would seek to start sending out missionaries under its auspices. Hudson now informed the society's executive committee of his intention to pursue further education in London in preparation for missionary service to China. Having an interest in him as a prospective CES representative, the committee offered to help with his living expenses in London. At the same time, his father made a similar offer.

Hudson wrote to the committee and his parents, thanking them for their generosity, telling each of the other's offer, and requesting a few days to pray about the matter. As he prayed, he came to the settled conviction that he should decline both offers! In that way he could further learn to depend solely on the Lord, as he knew he would often need to do in China.

Again he wrote to his parents and the CES committee to respectfully decline their offered support. He knew that each would suppose that he had accepted the other's offer so that neither parents nor committee would be anxious about his welfare.

When Hudson arrived in London late in September, he made his way to his uncle Benjamin's residence on Church Street, Soho. In a short while he accepted his cousin Tom's offer to share his room (and the expense to rent it) in the boardinghouse where he was staying nearby. Tom was the younger brother of John Hodson who had earlier stayed with the Taylors in Barnsley. At the end of October, Hudson began his training at the London Hospital in Whitechapel.

"When you move to London," Mrs. Finch had asked Hudson before he left Hull, "would you do me a favor?"

"Certainly if I'm able," responded Hudson.

"Each month half my husband's salary is sent to the London shipping office, then forwarded to me here. But there's a commission to pay for each delivery. Would you be so kind as to pick up the check each month and mail it to me yourself? I would be grateful, as that would save me a considerable amount."

Hudson readily agreed to this. One month, after he had been in London for some time, Mrs. Finch wrote requesting that he collect and send her husband's salary as quickly as possible. Her rent would soon be due, and her funds were nearly depleted.

Her request came at an inconvenient time for Hudson. In addition to his long hours of training at the hospital, he was studying intently for an examination through which he hoped to earn a scholarship. He happened to have on hand enough money of his own to cover the amount to be forwarded to Mrs. Finch. So he sent her his own funds, planning to reimburse himself when he picked up the captain's salary after the exam.

The medical school ended up closing for one day before the examination on account of the funeral of the Duke of Wellington. Hudson took advantage of the unexpected time off to hasten to the shipping office. But there a rude surprise awaited him.

"I'm so sorry, but I cannot pay that salary," a clerk informed Hudson. "It appears the officer in question has run away from his ship and gone to the gold diggings."

"Well," Hudson responded with some dismay, "that is very inconvenient for me! I have already advanced the money, and I know his wife will have no means of repaying it."

"I truly am sorry," the clerk said sincerely. "But of course I can only act according to orders. I'm afraid there's no help for you in this direction."

As Hudson further considered this unexpected turn of events during the walk back to his residence, he came to be at peace again. "I'm depending on the Lord for everything," he thought, "and His means are not limited. It is a small matter to be brought a little sooner than later into the position of needing fresh supplies from Him. He will surely continue to supply all my needs as He always has."

That same evening was when Hudson pricked his finger with a needle while sewing together a notebook for use at the London Hospital. The very next day he contracted the malignant fever that very nearly ended his life.

It was not until a few weeks later that he was able to leave his bedroom in the attic of the boardinghouse and be helped downstairs to the parlor. The doctor who had been attending to his recuperation happened to stop by to visit him that day.

"Well, Hudson!" he exclaimed when he spotted him lying on the sofa, "I didn't expect to find you down here."

"Tom helped me down," Hudson said with a weak smile, feeling exhausted from the exertion.

"I'm surprised you were able to do it, even with assistance," the doctor remarked. Then he advised, "Now the best thing you can do is to get off to the country as soon as you feel equal to the journey. You must rusticate until you have recovered a fair amount of health and strength. For if you begin your work too soon the consequences may still be serious."

After the doctor left, Hudson started praying about the advice that he had just received. Presently and surprisingly, it seemed as if God was directing him to the conclusion that he should return to the shipping office to inquire again about the wages that he had been unable to collect earlier.

"But, Lord," Hudson prayed further, "I cannot afford to take a conveyance. And it does not seem at all likely that I'll succeed in getting the money even if I do go. Oh, God, is not this impulse a mere clutching at a straw? Is this some trick of my own imagination rather than Your guidance and teaching?" As he continued to pray about the matter, however, he felt certain that God was indeed prompting him to go to the shipping office.

"But how am I to go?" he wondered. "I had to seek help just to get downstairs. And the shipping office is at least two miles away."

Vividly the scriptural assurance was brought to his mind that whatever he asked of God in the name of Christ would be done, that the Father might be glorified in the Son. He felt certain that what he needed to do was to seek strength for the long walk, to receive it by faith, and to set out on the journey in faith.

Without further hesitation, he prayed, "Lord, I am quite willing to take the walk if You will give me the strength." Then he sent the servant up to his room for his hat and walking stick.

Very slowly, Hudson made his way outside and started down the street. Never before had he shown such interest in the shop windows along the way. Every few steps he welcomed the opportunity to lean against the plate glass and examine the contents of a window while catching his breath. Proceeding at this snail's pace, he eventually succeeded in reaching the shipping office in the district of Cheapside.

There he sat down, utterly spent, at the base of the steps that led up to the first floor where he needed to go. He felt peculiar sitting there with men rushing up and down the stairs looking quizzically at him. No one stopped to offer assistance.

After a brief rest and another prayer for further strength, Hudson was able to ascend the staircase. Upon entering the shipping office he was delighted to find the clerk with whom he had spoken earlier. The man remembered him and, seeing that he looked pale and exhausted, inquired with evident concern about his health.

"I'm afraid I've had quite a serious illness," Hudson stated simply. "The doctor has ordered me to the country. But I thought it well to call here first and make further inquiry, lest there has been any mistake about the mate having run off to the gold diggings."

"Oh, I am so glad you have come," the clerk enthused, "for it turns out that it was an able seaman of the same name that ran away. The mate is still on board. The ship has just reached Gravesend, and will be up very soon. I shall be glad to give you the half-pay up to date, for doubtless it will reach his wife more safely through you. We all know what temptations beset the men when they arrive at home after a voyage."

Then, unexpectedly, the clerk said, "Before I give you that, however, step inside and share my lunch with me." Hudson started to decline, but the man insisted: "I was just about to eat, and you look like you could use some food and rest yourself."

Hudson accepted his kind offer with gratitude. He also silently thanked God for faithfully providing all his needs. After lunch, he slowly made his way back down the stairs and out onto the street. With the Lord's fresh financial provision in his pocket, he felt justified in paying the small fee to ride the omnibus back to Soho.

The next morning Hudson felt much better. He even ventured out again, this time making his way to the office of the doctor who had been caring for him. Though his uncle Benjamin was willing to pay his medical bill, Hudson felt that he should care for it now that the Lord had provided him with some money. When he inquired about his account, the physician refused to charge him because he was a medical student. He did allow Hudson to pay him eight shillings to cover the cost of the quinine that had been used in his treatment.

Having done so, Hudson saw that he had just enough money left over to buy a ticket to return home to Barnsley. He could plainly see that God had once again provided all his needs perfectly.

Hudson knew the physician was a skeptic toward spiritual matters, but he was so thrilled with the Lord's obvious activity in his life that he said: "Sir, I should very much like to speak to you freely, if I might do so without offense. I feel that under God I owe my life to your kind and capable care. And I wish very earnestly that you yourself might become a partaker of the same precious faith that I possess—a faith which would provide you with eternal life."

He continued on to relate his reason for being in London and how he had been depending on God alone rather than his parents or missions society to provide all his needs. He divulged the guidance the Lord had given him through prayer the day before as he lay on the parlor couch and the fact that, in faith, he had acted on that prompting by walking to Cheapside.

"Impossible!" the surgeon broke in at that point. "Why, I left you lying there more like a ghost than a man."

"I assure you, sir, that I really did undertake that walk. I was strengthened by the faith which God gave me to do so." Hudson then told him of the Lord's provision that had been awaiting him at the shipping office. "And look!" he concluded, showing the doctor the money left in his possession. "After paying all my outstanding bills, I have just enough remaining to take me home to Yorkshire and to provide me with needed refreshment along the way."

The physician was deeply touched by Hudson's earnest testimony. Tears misted his eyes and he said, "I would give all the world for a faith like yours."

"You may have such a faith," Hudson told him. "It is obtained without money and without price. All you need to do is place your complete trust in Christ."

Hudson never saw that doctor again. When he returned to London from Barnsley, he learned that the surgeon had suffered a stroke and had gone to the country to convalesce, but had never rallied. Hudson was unable to learn the physician's spiritual condition when he died, but he always hoped that the Lord had used his witness to draw the man to saving faith in Jesus Christ.

The day after his visit with the doctor, Hudson returned home to Barnsley. There his parents were shocked to find him in such a weakened condition. When he was well enough to return to London, they made him promise that he would not attempt again to live on such a severely restricted diet.

Hudson returned to London in January of 1853. That winter and early spring proved to be a discouraging time for him. His cousin, Tom, was ill with rheumatic fever, and Hudson spent many late nights nursing him back to health.

Worst of all for Hudson at that time were concerns that weighed on his heart regarding his relationship with Marianne Vaughan. For three years he had cherished the hope that she would consent to marry him and share his life of missionary service in China. They had even recently become formally engaged, but Hudson began to notice that each time he tried to arrange a meeting with Marianne, she always had some excuse for why she could not come.

Finally he endeavored to have a frank talk with her. She divulged: "My mother is ill. Father is worried that she may die at any time and that I'll go with you to China. He gave his consent to our engagement, but I know he's most unhappy. I feel like I'm in a terrible dilemma."

Hudson suggested that they write her father to determine his true feelings about their proposed marriage. The reply he received from Mr. Vaughan was crushing: "Were you to remain in England, nothing would give me more pleasure than to see you happily united to Marianne. Though I do not forbid your connection, I feel I can never willingly give her up, or ever think of her leaving this country." Thus it was mutually agreed that their engagement should be dissolved.

At the end of March, Hudson accepted the offer to become the assistant to a surgeon, Dr. Thomas Brown, in the Bishopsgate region of London. Under this arrangement, he boarded with Dr. Brown and his family. He continued to attend morning and early afternoon classes at the London Hospital, which was only two miles from his new residence. His late afternoons and evenings were devoted to assisting Dr. Brown in a variety of duties.

One of the patients whom Hudson treated during those days was an avowed atheist who was dying of gangrene. It was Hudson's daily duty to dress the infected foot. The man, who was vehemently antagonistic toward anything religious, had not entered a church since his wedding day forty years earlier. Recently when a Christian layman came to read Scriptures to him, he flew into a rage and ordered the well-meaning individual out of his room. When the local vicar called on him, the man spit in his face and refused to allow him to speak.

Hudson was deeply concerned about the man's eternal welfare, but did not broach spiritual matters the first two or three days he attended him. Through Hudson's physical care the man's suffering was eased somewhat and he began to express appreciation to the young medical student.

Then came the day when Hudson screwed up his courage and talked with his patient about his grave condition and his need for the Savior. The man's countenance betrayed obvious annoyance, but instead of bursting out at Hudson he rolled over in bed with his back toward him and refused to say another word. This same response was elicited on future occasions whenever Hudson sought to share a spiritually beneficial word with him.

Hudson often thought about and prayed for him throughout those days. Eventually his heart began to sink, as it seemed his efforts were accomplishing no good and might actually be having the opposite effect of further hardening the man.

Finally one day Hudson could contain himself no longer. As he prepared to leave the patient's room he paused at the doorway, then suddenly burst into tears. Crossing to the dying man's bedside, he exclaimed: "My friend, whether you will hear or whether you will forbear, I *must* deliver my soul. How I wish you would allow me to pray with you."

The man was completely taken aback and stammered, "W-Well if it will be a relief to you, then do."

Immediately Hudson fell to his knees and poured out his soul to God in behalf of the ailing man. "Then and there, I believe," Hudson recorded later, "the Lord wrought a change in his soul. He was never afterwards unwilling to be spoken to and prayed with, and within a few days he definitely accepted Christ as his Savior. Oh the joy it was to me to see that dear man rejoicing in hope of the glory of God!" He further reflected on this incident:

> I have often thought since, in connection with this case and the work of God generally, of the words, "He that goeth forth *weeping*, bearing precious seed, shall doubtless come again rejoicing, bringing his sheaves with him." Perhaps if there were more of that intense distress for souls that leads to tears, we should more frequently see the results we desire. Sometimes it may be that while we are complaining of the hardness of the hearts of those we are seeking to benefit, the hardness of our own hearts and our own feeble apprehension of the solemn reality of eternal things may be the true cause of our want of success.

There was intense interest among Christians that spring over developments in China where the Taiping Rebellion was underway. The leader of the rebellion, Hong Xiuquan, was a professing Christian who had studied the Bible under an American missionary, Issacher Roberts. Hong's forces were intent on overthrowing the lazy and oppressive imperial Manchu government as well as abolishing idol worship and the opium trade.

In addition, the Taipings seemed very open and positive in their outlook toward foreigners. When in March of 1853 the Taiping army captured Nanking, the former capital of the Chinese empire and the key to the country's main north-south waterway, excitement ran high among Western Christians that perhaps very soon all of China would be opened to the gospel.

That same spring Hudson Taylor was wrestling with an important decision. The Chinese Evangelization Society had indicated a willingness to cover his remaining educational expenses so that he could become an MD and a member of the Royal College of Surgeons (MRCS). But if the Lord called him to go to China he desired to be free to do so immediately. Once in China, he did not want to be obligated to doing hospital work for a human agency should God direct him into itinerate evangelism ministry in the interior of the country. In May he wrote the CES to respectfully decline the generous offer and sought to explain his rationale for doing so.

On Saturday, June 4, Charles Bird, the secretary of the CES, sat at his desk, penning a letter to Hudson Taylor. In part it read:

My Dear Sir—As you have fully made up your mind to go to China, and also not to qualify as a Surgeon, I would affectionately suggest that you lose no time in preparing to start. At this time we want really devoted men, and I believe your heart is right before God and your motives pure, so that you need not hesitate in offering. If you think it right to offer yourself, I shall be most happy to lay your application before the Board.

The letter was just completed and still lying on Bird's desk when a knock came at the door and in stepped Hudson. "Why, I have just been writing to you!" exclaimed the secretary. "The letter is not yet posted."

He shared the contents of the letter with Hudson. A long, serious discussion followed in which Hudson expressed his concerns and Bird allayed those fears. Hudson promptly submitted a formal application to the CES committee. Three weeks later the CES informed him that it was ready to send him to China as one of its agents as soon as he could make the necessary arrangements for the journey.

6

A Perilous Voyage
to China

On Monday, September 19, 1853, the twenty-three-member crew of the *Dumfries*, a small three-masted ship bound for China, scurried to complete its final preparations before the voyage began. The clipper was all but ready to pull away from the dock at Liverpool.

Hudson and his mother sat in the stern's cabin, which would be his home for the next six months. James and Amelia Taylor had both come to Liverpool the previous week to see their son off. The scheduled departure of the *Dumfries* had been delayed several days, so Hudson's father had been forced to return to his business in Barnsley.

Now mother and son sat beside each other on the bed, sharing their final moments together. Both realized that it would likely be a very long time until they would see each other again and that perhaps their reunion would be in heaven rather than on earth.

They sang a hymn together and then prayed. Hudson's tone of voice was composed and joyous until he prayed, "And now, God, I commend to Your care the objects of my love—Father and Mother, sister Amelia . . ."

His voice faltered and he paused to regain his composure, then continued, concluding confidently: "Heavenly Father, I realize that I am entering upon a course of trial, difficulty, and danger. Yet none of these things move me, neither count I my life dear unto myself, so that I might finish my course with joy, and the ministry which I have received of the Lord Jesus, to testify the gospel of the grace of God."

After Hudson read a psalm they went on deck. The ship had already been loosed from its moorings, so Mrs. Taylor was helped ashore. She sat down on a beam of timber on the dock's edge and, feeling suddenly chilled, began to tremble all over. Hudson quickly stepped onto the dock and sat down beside her.

He lovingly drew her close to him and sought to comfort her: "Dear Mother, do not weep. It is but for a little while, and we shall meet again. Think of the glorious object I have in leaving you. It is not for wealth or fame, but to try to bring the poor Chinese to the knowledge of Jesus."

Hudson was obliged to return to the ship. Once again he grasped his mother's hand, this time over the ship's edge. "Farewell, Mother," he stated earnestly. "God bless you."

"And God bless you, my son," she responded.

She walked along beside the ship until it passed through the gate at the end of the dock. Suddenly a piercing cry of anguish escaped from her aching heart. Said Hudson later of that cry: "It went through me like a knife. I never knew so fully, until then, what 'God *so* loved the world' meant. And I am quite sure my precious mother learned more of the love of God for the perishing in that one hour than in all her life before."

He climbed into the ship's rigging and waved his hat in final farewell. His mother in turn stood at the end of the dock and waved her handkerchief. Within a few minutes the ship disappeared over the horizon.

Almost immediately the *Dumfries* encountered a westerly gale as it headed out into the Irish Sea. All through that first week it tacked back and forth but made little progress. By Sunday the winds had reached near hurricane force as the ship attempted to maneuver around the northwest coast of Wales.

The middle of that afternoon Hudson struggled on deck to find the angry sea white with foam. The waves rose like hills on either side of the ship, looking like they might swamp it at any moment. The fierce westerly wind pushed the ship incessantly toward the Welsh coast.

"I've never seen a wilder sea," Captain Morris, himself a Christian, divulged to Hudson. "Unless God help us, there is no hope."

"How far might we be from the coast?" Hudson queried.

"Fifteen or sixteen miles," the captain responded. "We can do nothing but carry all possible sail. The more we carry the less we drift. It is for our lives. God grant the timbers may bear it."

The captain then had a second sail hoisted on each mast. The ship tore through the water at a frightening pace. One moment it was perched high atop a gigantic wave, the next it plunged headlong into the trough of the sea as though it might go direct to the bottom. The ship's windward side rose dangerously high while seawater sometimes poured over its lee side.

As Hudson watched the sunset that day he thought: "Tomorrow you will rise as usual. But unless the Lord works miraculously on our behalf a few broken timbers will be all that is left of us and our ship."

He began to be enveloped by a sense of loneliness and started feeling very anxious. "Should the Dumfries be lost," he reflected, "my dear loved ones will have to endure such sorrow. And what of the expense to the Society? It paid nearly a hundred pounds for my passage and outfit for this journey. What of the unprepared state of the crew? These men are not ready to step into eternity."

At his next thought a chill ran through his body: "And what about the coldness of the water and the struggle of death? I have not the slightest doubt about the eternal happiness which awaits me in heaven. I do not dread death itself. But death under such circumstances?!"

He went to his cabin and read a couple of hymns, some psalms, and John 13–14. After that he felt comforted and actually fell asleep for an hour. When he awoke, he went back up on deck.

"Can we clear Holyhead?" he asked the captain.

"If we make no leeway, we may just do it. But if we drift, God help us!"

The ship did continue to drift. At first the Holyhead lighthouse shone brightly dead ahead of the ship; then it could be seen on the ship's outward side. The vessel was on a collision course with the shoreline.

Hudson returned to his cabin. Taking out his pocketbook, he wrote his name and home address in it, in case he was drowned and his body was recovered. He also tied a few belongings in a hamper that he thought would float and perhaps help him or someone else to land.

"God my Father," he prayed, "I commend my soul to You and my friends to Your care. If it be possible, may this cup pass from us. Lord, have mercy on us and spare us, for the sake of the unconverted crew members as well as for Your own glory as the God who hears and answers prayer."

Suddenly the words of Psalm 50:15 came to his mind: "And call upon me in the day of trouble: I will deliver thee, and thou shalt glorify me."

"God, I plead with you to fulfill this promise in our behalf," Hudson fervently prayed. "Nevertheless, Father, I submit myself to Your perfect will, whatever that may be."

Returning to the deck once again, Hudson posed another question to Captain Morris: "Could the lifeboats survive in such a sea?"

"No," came the straightforward response. Then the captain had a searching question of his own for Hudson: "We cannot live half an hour now. So what of your call to labor for the Lord in China?"

Hudson's anxiety had melted away. He was able to answer the captain's query with genuine joy in his heart: "I would not wish to be in any other position. I still strongly expect to reach China. But if matters turn out otherwise, the Master will say it was well that I was found seeking to obey His command."

A moment later Captain Morris stated: "We must try to turn her and tack, or all is over. The sea may sweep the deck in turning and wash everything overboard, but we must try."

He gave the order to turn the ship out to sea, but the attempt failed. Then he ordered the vessel to be turned in the opposite direction. This maneuver succeeded, though barely, as the craft passed within two ships' length of the rocks along the shore. Just then the wind shifted two points in their favor, enabling them to make their way out of the bay.

A week later the *Dumfries* ran into another stretch of rough weather while navigating through the Bay of Biscay off the west coast of France. At one point the rough sea nearly swamped the ship. Three weeks from the time they left Liverpool, however, they had reached safer waters.

As the ship neared the equator it encountered an opposite sailing difficulty—becalmed waters. For days on end there would be very little wind. Usually a light breeze would start up shortly after sunset and would continue until dawn. But during the day the ship would lay with its sails flapping limply, often drifting back in a current and losing much of the distance that had been gained the previous night. Sometimes the listless vessel was able to make only six or seven miles of progress in a twenty-four-hour period.

Hudson asked the captain's permission to begin holding regular religious services for the crew. He was supported in this desire by the ship's steward and carpenter who, like the captain, were Christians. These services were favorably received, especially during the long, monotonous days they experienced while in calms. During the course of the twenty-three-week journey, Hudson was able to lead sixty of these devotional services.

The *Dumfries* rounded the Cape of Good Hope on the southern tip of Africa early in December. Christmas Day was celebrated by killing and feasting on one of the pigs that the ship carried. Slowly they progressed toward the East Indian islands, often encountering becalmed weather conditions.

Sunday, January 29, 1854, found the ship once again helpless in a still sea, not many miles off the coast of northern Papua New Guinea. As Hudson led the worship service that morning on the deck, he noticed that Captain Morris looked troubled and frequently went to look out over the side of the ship.

After the service he asked the captain the cause for his concern and was told, "A current of four knots is carrying us toward sunken reefs on the shoreline. We're already so near, it's improbable that we'll get through the afternoon in safety."

After the noontime dinner the entire crew got into a longboat and attempted to turn the bow of the ship into the current in order to reduce its rate of drift and lessen its eventual force of impact. When this effort failed, the captain stood on the deck in silence for a long time, then stated, "Well, we have done everything that can be done. We can only await the result."

Presently a thought occurred to Hudson, and he said, "No, there is one thing we have not done yet."

"What is that?" questioned the captain dubiously.

"Four of us on board are Christians," suggested Hudson. "Let us each retire to his own cabin, and in agreed prayer ask the Lord to give us immediately a breeze. He can as easily send it now as at sunset."

Captain Morris was quiet a moment, then responded: "Agreed. You go and share this plan with the other two men. I'll go to my cabin and commence praying."

Hudson spoke with the steward and the carpenter, then retired to his cabin to beseech the Lord. He had a good but very brief season of prayer, then felt so certain that their request had been granted that he could not continue asking.

Shortly he went back on deck and approached the first officer, a godless man, stating simply, "Sir, might I request that you let down the corners of the mainsail?" These had been drawn up in order to lessen the useless flapping of the sail against the rigging.

"What would be the good of that?" the officer responded roughly.

"Some of us have been in prayer," explained Hudson calmly and confidently, "asking God to send a wind. I believe it is coming immediately. And we're so near to the reef by this time that there's not a minute to lose."

The seasoned sailor looked at the young missionary with contempt and swore. "I would rather see a wind than hear of it," he growled.

Despite himself, however, he looked up to the topmost sail. The corner of it was beginning to flutter in the breeze.

"Don't you see the wind is coming?" Hudson exclaimed. "Look at the royal!"

"No, it's only a cat's paw," countered the sailor, using a term that meant a mere puff of wind.

"Cat's paw or not," insisted Hudson, "pray let down the mainsail and give us the full benefit."

The officer did not hesitate further. He gave the order and crew members scurried to carry it out. The sound of the sudden activity on the deck brought the captain out of his cabin to see what was happening. He was astounded to see that the breeze had indeed come.

Within minutes the ship was making its way safely back out to sea at six or seven knots. The remainder of its voyage was completed in relative safety. Five more weeks passed until the *Dumfries* docked in Shanghai, China, where Hudson would face even greater peril.

7

A Distressful Beginning in China

Late in February of 1854, more than five months after setting sail from Liverpool, the *Dumfries* arrived at Gutzlaff Island near the mouth of the Yangtze estuary, fifteen miles from Shanghai. There it was detained by heavy fog. The English pilot of a nearby vessel boarded the *Dumfries* and received a hearty welcome.

He was full of news about startling changes that had taken place in China while Hudson had been at sea: "The Taiping Rebellion is devastating province after province as it progresses toward Peking. Even Shanghai is plunged in all the horrors of war. A local band of rebels—the Red Turbans—has taken possession of the city. An imperial army of forty to fifty thousand men is surrounding the city and has it under siege. The imperialists are a greater threat to the European settlement here than even the rebels themselves. Under such conditions you must also be prepared to find everything at famine prices."

Hudson Taylor first stepped onto Chinese soil late in the afternoon on Wednesday, March 1, 1854. "My feelings on stepping ashore," he later wrote, "I cannot attempt to describe. My heart felt as though it had not room and must burst its bonds, while tears of gratitude and thankfulness fell from my eyes."

He spotted his country's flag flying over the British consulate not far from the dock and quickly made his way there. He carried three letters of introduction addressed to specific missionaries in China whom it was thought might provide him with assistance in getting settled.

Hudson was keenly disappointed to learn that the missionary with whom he was best acquainted had been buried a month or two earlier, while he was still at sea. He further discovered that a second missionary to whom he had an introductory letter had recently left for America. His third letter had been given to him by a comparative stranger and was addressed to Dr. Walter Medhurst of the London Missionary Society (LMS). Hudson had expected less help from this contact, but now it was his only option.

Following directions provided him at the consulate, he made his way through narrow, muddy streets for over a mile to the LMS compound in the European settlement on the northern outskirts of the city. Stopping to inquire at one of the LMS residences, he was greeted by a small group of Chinese servants. They could not speak English and he was unable to understand a word of their particular dialect. He was relieved when he spotted a fellow European approaching.

"May I help you, sir?" the young Englishman of about thirty years of age asked in kindly fashion. Extending his hand, he introduced himself, "I'm Joseph Edkins."

"I'm much obliged to you, sir," Hudson responded, shaking the man's hand. "I'm Hudson Taylor of the Chinese Evangelization Society. I've just arrived and have a letter of introduction to Doctor Medhurst."

"He's no longer here in our compound," revealed Edkins. "Due to our dangerous proximity to the constant fighting at the city's north gate not far from here, it was thought best to have Doctor and Mrs. Medhurst move to the British consulate. However, Doctor William Lockhart, the surgeon at our hospital, remains here on the premises. Please come in and make yourself at home. I'll go find Doctor Lockhart and bring him to meet you."

When the surgeon arrived he, too, greeted Hudson warmly. He quickly perceived Hudson's need for immediate housing. "I'm afraid our settlement is so crowded that lodgings are not to be had at any price," Dr. Lockhart reported. "However, I'm living alone at present, as my wife has returned to England for a time. You're welcome to stay here as my guest until you're able to make other housing arrangements." Hudson gratefully accepted the doctor's generous offer on the condition that he would be permitted to pay a modest fee to cover his boarding expenses.

After breakfast the next morning Hudson returned to the consulate to collect any mail that had arrived for him. He was disappointed to find only one letter, but happily discovered that it contained enclosures from both his mother and sisters. He needed to pay two shillings postage for the single letter, the equivalent of about half his day's salary, but he assured them in his written response, "Never did I pay two shillings more willingly in my life than for that letter."

Later that day he attended the daily evangelistic service at the LMS hospital. There he heard Dr. Medhurst preach the gospel in the local Shanghai dialect to those who had come to receive medical treatment.

After the service, the renowned medical missionary counseled Hudson: "I would advise you to commence your language studies with the Mandarin dialect as it is the most widely spoken in China. I will undertake to procure a teacher for you."

Hudson was deeply grateful to Dr. Lockhart and the LMS for providing him with temporary quarters, but he soon became uncomfortable with this arrangement. The fact that he was being cared for by a missionary society to which he did not belong made him feel like an unfledged cuckoo—an intruder in another bird's nest.

Before the week was over, Hudson began to see the terrifying side of life in war-torn Shanghai. Sometimes guns fired all through the night. From his residence in the European settlement he could see the lights of the sentries at night as they patrolled the city wall less than half a mile away. Intense fighting was witnessed from his windows, with men being killed and wounded before his very eyes.

Excerpts from a letter that Hudson wrote to George Pearse of the CES just two days after he arrived in China reveal an overwhelming set of trials and complexities that immediately confronted him. Remembering that all of this came upon Hudson unexpectedly makes it easy to understand his distressed tone in this communication:

I felt very much disappointed on finding no letter from you, but I hope to receive one by next mail. Shanghai is in a very unsettled state, the Rebels and imperialists fighting continually. This morning a cannon fired near us awoke me before daybreak, shaking the house and making the windows rattle violently.

There is not a house to be obtained here, or even part of one; those not occupied by Europeans are filled with Chinese merchants who have left the city. The missionaries who were living in the city have had to leave, and are residing with others here in the settlement at present; so that had it not been for the kindness of Dr. Lockhart I should have been quite nonplussed. As it is, I scarcely know what to do. How long the present state of things may last it is impossible to say.

Please excuse this hasty, disconnected letter with all its faults. It is so cold just now that I can scarcely feel pen or paper. Everything is very dear, and fuel costs at times an almost fabulous price. Once more I must beg you to excuse this letter, and please reply with all possible expedition that I may know what to do.

Hudson was to receive a salary of eighty pounds (about four hundred American dollars at that time) from the CES for his first year of service in China. It quickly became apparent that such compensation was woefully inadequate. By comparison, single missionaries serving with other societies in Shanghai at the time received more than three times that amount in salary in addition to having their expenses paid for rent, medical treatment, procuring a Chinese teacher, and books. Though Hudson cared nothing about being equally compensated, he did at times suffer embarrassment over the fact that his clothes were noticeably shabby compared with those of his missionary acquaintances.

Hudson's first Sunday in China he attended two morning worship services held in the London Missionary Society compound. That afternoon he accompanied an LMS missionary, Alexander Wylie, in venturing into the city. Hudson watched as Wylie freely conversed with and distributed tracts to soldiers on the wall, people on the streets, and priests in the temples. The two missionaries observed rebel soldiers congregating at the west gate in preparation for launching a surprise offensive against the imperialist forces.

Hudson and Wylie made their way to the LMS chapel, which was inside the city. There Dr. Medhurst preached to a packed house, holding out to fearful people the hope of finding protective shelter in God. After the service, six bags of rice were distributed among the poor. This food distribution was done daily to deliver from starvation those who had no way of carrying out gainful employment under wartime conditions.

As Hudson and his fellow missionaries approached the north gate after the service, the fighting had grown fierce outside the city. One man was brought in dead while another was carried in who had been shot in the chest. Hudson examined a third man, who was in agony after a rifle ball passed clear through his arm, shattering the bone.

"We can do nothing for him unless he comes with us to the hospital," Dr. Lockhart stated gravely. "Otherwise his enemies will only pull our dressings off."

A little farther on, the missionaries passed a group of soldiers who were transporting a small cannon that they had captured in the battle. Next they encountered five prisoners being dragged along by their queues. The five, who doubtless were about to be decapitated, cried out piteously to the missionaries to save them, but they were powerless to interfere.

Hudson observed human suffering daily on a scale that surpassed anything he had ever before imagined. His mind was filled with horror at the tortures that soldiers in both armies inflicted on their prisoners and at the ravaging of citizens as the countryside was pillaged for supplies. His sensitive nature was traumatized by this living nightmare that he had been thrust into without adequate warning or preparation.

The futile idolatrous heathenism that pervaded the city further oppressed his spirit. Many of the temples had been completely or partially destroyed and the idols damaged in the fighting. It was evident that the gods were not able to protect even themselves under these circumstances. Yet the desperate people, thinking they had nowhere else to turn for help, kept worshiping them and crying out to them for deliverance.

Hudson's anxiety over this was compounded by the fact that he was unable to speak the language of the people to share with them the peace and security to be found in having a personal relationship with the one true God of the Bible. Ever since his own conversion five years earlier he had faithfully and readily proclaimed the gospel. Now he was deeply distressed at being unable to share the message of eternal life through faith in Jesus Christ with those all around him who daily lived under the threat of death.

Such a circumstance did motivate him to begin his Mandarin studies in earnest. As soon as a teacher was available, Hudson devoted a minimum of five hours per day to language study.

He was neither university trained nor connected with a prominent denomination as were his LMS acquaintances. His position as a missionary was unusual and open to criticism. He planned to do medical work, but he was not a doctor. He was accustomed to preaching and providing pastoral care, yet he was not ordained, and he steadfastly refused the title "Reverend" that others were inclined to give him.

Hudson soon learned that the objectives and methods of his supporting society were viewed as unrealistic or even absurd by experienced, practical missionaries on the field. In fact, the CES and its monthly publication, *The Gleaner*, were considerably ridiculed in Shanghai. It was extremely painful to Hudson to hear his fellow missionaries tearing apart the ideals and perspectives set forth in each new issue of *The Gleaner*.

He was both surprised and troubled by what he perceived to be worldly tendencies on the part of many in Shanghai's missionary community. Missionaries had extensive interaction with government officials and military officers stationed in Shanghai, being very useful to them as interpreters. This intercourse promoted considerable secular socializing and an undue interest in status and fashion that struck Hudson as being inappropriate for Christian missionaries.

His first weeks and months in Shanghai were dangerous ones for him and the other missionaries because of the wartime conditions that surrounded them. Preparing to leave the city one day through the east gate, Hudson and Alexander Wylie stopped to converse with two coolies, a term meaning unskilled laborer or porter hired at low or subsistence wages. Suddenly the imperialists launched an artillery attack from their batteries on the opposite side of the river. Hudson and Wylie, hearing the whiz of cannonballs unpleasantly near, hastily retreated to a safer location. Unfortunately, the coolies lingered at the gate too long and were seriously injured.

The two missionaries hastened to the European settlement where they stopped for a few minutes at a store to make a purchase before proceeding to the mission compound. There, at the door of the hospital, they found the two coolies with whom they had conversed. All four of their ankles had been shattered by a cannonball.

Amputation was recommended as it was the only hope of saving the men's lives. When they refused that extreme treatment, infection set in and they both died. Hudson and Wylie were struck by the narrowness of their own escape on that occasion.

One morning Hudson and another missionary were conversing on a veranda in the compound as a battle raged about three-quarters of a mile away from them. Suddenly a stray cannonball flew right between them and, with a thunderous crash, buried itself in the veranda wall.

On April 4, after Hudson had been in China for just over a month, the battle of Muddy Flat was fought. This involved an armed conflict between foreign troops and imperialist soldiers.

For weeks the imperial forces had become increasingly menacing toward foreigners, whose presence they resented as interfering with their efforts to recapture Shanghai. Imperialists set up their camps and artillery closer and closer to the European settlement. Alarmed, the consuls united in insisting that imperial forces must withdraw to a greater distance.

Early in the morning on April 4, imperial war junks began moving downstream toward the settlement where British, French, and American frigates lay. They were commanded to stop. When they refused to obey, a British ship opened fire on them.

Meanwhile the British consul, Rutherford Alcock, issued an ultimatum to the commander of the imperial forces: "If you do not begin to move your troops by three p.m. today, our marines will come ashore; If your men have not withdrawn by four p.m., they will be driven out and their camps destroyed."

Three and then four o'clock saw no movement on the part of the imperial troops. British and American marines along with merchant sailors went ashore and, under Alcock's command, fired on the imperialists. The imperial soldiers at first returned fire, but soon began to flee in all directions.

Suddenly hundreds of Red Turbans appeared on the scene as rebel soldiers poured out of Shanghai to take advantage of the situation. As British and American marines began burning the deserted campsites, rebel soldiers helped themselves to the arms and ammunition left behind by the imperialists.

After this battle, relations between imperialists and foreigners were so strained that, for a time, the latter hardly dared to venture out of the European settlement. At first it was feared that

73

reprisals might be carried out against foreigners, but instead the frustrated imperial soldiers vented their wrath on helpless citizens in the surrounding villages.

All this had a definite negative impact for Hudson Taylor and the other missionaries. For several weeks their ministry activities among the natives were largely curtailed and had to be confined to the boundaries of the settlement. An itinerating preaching venture to outlying villages that Hudson and another missionary had been planning needed to be postponed for the time being.

8

Living among the Chinese

A s Hudson's first spring in China gave way to summer, he continued to prosecute his study of the Chinese language with all diligence despite the ongoing war and the oncoming heat. In addition to maintaining his discipline of devoting a minimum of five hours daily to learning the Mandarin dialect, he also spent time studying medicine, chemistry, Greek, and Latin. "But the sweetest duties of the day," he wrote to his beloved sister, Amelia, "are those that lead to Jesus— prayer, reading, and meditation upon His precious Word."

June brought intense heat and humidity. For weeks on end the temperature climbed above one hundred degrees during the day and did not drop below eighty degrees at night. The stifling heat and prolific mosquitoes made it difficult to sleep. Hudson's eyes burned much of the time and he experienced frequent headaches, doubtless from a combination of prolonged studies and inadequate sleep.

He was also quite lonely. While he was with his Chinese teacher during the day, his evenings were generally spent alone in writing or study. He was developing a meaningful friendship with another young missionary, John Burdon of the Church Missionary Society, but he was sensitive to the fact that he must not take too much of John's time as he was married and had other friends. Witnessing the love and happiness that John enjoyed with his wife underscored the loneliness Hudson felt without such a companion to share life.

To make matters worse, throughout June and July Hudson received no letters from family members or friends back home. Letters had been mailed to him that should have arrived then, but some were not delivered until much later while others were lost.

That summer he was startled to learn that the CES had sent out more missionaries to Shanghai. Dr. William Parker, a Scottish physician, and his family had already set sail and would be arriving in a few months. Hudson received this news through a roundabout source rather than directly from his supporting society.

He was delighted at the prospect of having other CES missionaries on the field with him but deeply perplexed over how to make appropriate preparations for their arrival. Since he had not been able to procure housing for himself, how could he possibly do so for a family of five? Anxiously he waited for letters from the CES committee appraising him of the situation and instructing him what to do, but none ever arrived.

Finally he concluded that he must make another attempt at locating a property to rent, although the likelihood of finding one seemed extremely remote. Surprisingly, within a few days he discovered an available house just outside the north gate of the city. The structure had been built in a rather ramshackle fashion, but it was spacious, with five rooms upstairs and seven down.

The house was in a less secure spot, being located in a neighborhood of native dwellings between the European settlement and the city's northern wall. Of this he wrote to a friend:

> The Chinese house to which I am removing is in a dangerous position, being beyond the protection of the settlement and liable to injury from both imperialists and rebels. The former have threatened to burn the street, and the latter have two cannon constantly pointing at it. At any rate I am thankful that my way is hedged up on every side, so that no choice is left me. I am obliged to go forward. And if you hear of my being killed or injured, do not think it a pity that I came, but thank God I was permitted to distribute some Scriptures and tracts and to speak a few words in broken Chinese for Him who died for me.

On August 30 Hudson was able to move to his new residence. His Mandarin teacher was unwilling to enter that dangerous neighborhood, so Hudson hired, instead, a native to teach him the Shanghai dialect. That teacher, Mr. Si, proved to be a great blessing from the Lord, as he was a committed Christian who capably assisted Hudson in a number of ways.

Word spread of Hudson's medical knowledge, and soon he was seeing several patients each day. He also started a day school, taught by Mr. Si, which quickly attracted nearly a score of pupils. On several occasions Hudson and Si ventured into the city to distribute New Testaments and other Christian literature.

In mid-September Hudson and two other missionaries—Joseph Edkins and John Quarterman, an American Presbyterian—made a daytime excursion down the Huangpu River to the city of Woosung. They distributed Scriptures and tracts on numerous junks, receiving promises from the captains to whom they were given that they would not only be read but also passed along to acquaintances in distant ports.

As the missionaries returned home that evening in the deepening darkness, they began to puzzle over how they could safely pass the imperial warships that guarded the river at Shanghai. If they were mistaken for rebel spies, they would doubtless be fired upon.

"I propose that we sing as we pass them," suggested Edkins, "so that they will know we are foreigners."

This they did, lustily singing several hymns as they floated past some ships they thought to be the armed fleet. They were just about to congratulate each other on having accomplished their objective when suddenly the boatmen guiding their small craft began shouting at them to start singing again. What they had mistakenly supposed was the imperial fleet was not, and they were just now coming within range of its guns.

Quickly they joined together in singing loudly another hymn. Unfortunately the last refrain died out just as they came abreast the largest ship of the fleet. All at once an alarm gong was sounded on the big warship.

"What next?" cried Edkins. "There is not a moment to lose!"

He immediately launched into a song that Hudson did not know. Quarterman started belting out an American tune with which he was also unfamiliar, "Blow Ye the Trumpet, Blow!" Hudson raised a third song with all the volume he could muster. Men on the warship began shouting, and the crew of Hudson's boat yelled more loudly still, trying to explain who they were. Suddenly the whole situation struck Hudson as being so ludicrous that he burst into a fit of laughter that he later said was "most inappropriate to the occasion."

A threatening inquiry was shouted from the imperial ship: "Who goes there?"

"White devils," yelled back the frantic boatmen.

"Great English nation," hollered Hudson and Edkins in unison.

"Flowery flag country," cried Quarterman, using the descriptive Chinese phrase for America.

After further explanation they were allowed to pass. Edkins and Quarterman then began to lecture the crew members for having called them white devils.

The boatmen, who had not yet been paid for their day's work and who doubtless feared they were in danger of losing at least a portion of their wages for having offended the missionaries, were most apologetic: "Most honorable sirs," they claimed, "we were so frightened that we really did not know what we were saying. We will be most careful to refrain from such offensive expressions in the future."

That same month Hudson shared in the deep sorrow that came into the home of his good friend John Burdon. Mrs. Burdon had not been well since giving birth to a daughter three months earlier. Then she became gravely ill with cholera. Hudson spent much time at the Burdons', assisting John who had become worn out from anxiety and the heavy responsibility of caring for his wife and daughter. When Mrs. Burdon died on September 26, Hudson made all the funeral arrangements for the grieving young widower.

As October wore on, Hudson's location in the Chinese neighborhood just outside the city wall became increasingly precarious. Daily skirmishes took place between imperial and rebel forces. One noon a large cannonball struck the roof of Hudson's house, breaking some tiles, and fell at the feet of his teacher's child who was standing in a doorway. "Had he been half a yard farther out," Hudson informed his parents in a letter, "it must have killed him."

Hudson was awakened the next night by a nearby fire. Dressing quickly, he went up on the roof of his house to assess the situation. Just four or five doors up the street an entire building was engulfed in flames. The wind was strong that night, and he feared it could easily spread the fire to other wooden structures, including his own home, in the tightly compacted neighborhood. He began to pray urgently for protection. Presently it started raining, the wind decreased, and the fire died out.

While he was there on the roof, several bullets struck the surrounding houses. Two or three ricocheted off the tiles of his own roof. Finally a large cannonball, weighing four or five pounds, crashed into the ridge of the home next door, showering him with tile fragments. He hastily retreated back inside his house.

With the Parkers due to arrive at any time, Hudson was again at a loss concerning what to do about their housing. It was obvious that they could not safely be brought to the quarters he had been renting in the Chinese district.

Then, at the end of October, John Burdon decided to vacate the home on the LMS compound that had become such a place of sadness to him. Hudson was given the opportunity to lease the residence and did so, paying the first installment of rent out of his own meager funds. He further had the opportunity to sublet half the premises to an American missionary family that was also in need of shelter. This he did in exchange for half the rental expense.

Eventually conditions became so dangerous in the Chinese neighborhood that Hudson concluded he could not continue to live there. Reluctantly he left the schoolchildren and neighbors to whom he had been ministering and moved to his newly rented residence on the mission compound. God's providential watchful care in that decision soon became readily apparent. Even before he was able to retrieve all his possessions from the native house, it was set ablaze during yet another skirmish and burned to the ground.

The Parkers arrived just two days after Hudson returned to the LMS compound. While he was thrilled to have CES associates with him on the field, he was embarrassed over the cramped and sparsely furnished living quarters he had to offer them. A six-room house was hardly adequate for two families with young children and a single man to share. Hudson had almost no furnishings for the Parkers, his only possessions being two or three square tables, half a dozen chairs, and a Chinese bed. These he happily laid at their disposal, but he was painfully aware that so much more was needed.

Matters were worsened for him when other missionaries began calling on the Parkers and observed their straitened living conditions. These visitors were not hesitant in voicing their criticisms of what they perceived to be Hudson's negligence in failing to make proper provisions for the Parkers.

Hudson's critics, of course, were unaware of the attendant circumstances of the case, and he refused to divulge these in order to safeguard the reputation of his sponsoring society. He did not explain that in order simply to lease the house he had been forced to far exceed the expenditure limits that the CES had set for him. Nor did he reveal that after paying the first installment of rent out of his own resources, he had been left with only three dollars, enough to cover one week's expenses. He also kept to himself the fact that the CES had inadvertently failed to send a letter of credit that had been promised Dr. Parker to cover the expenses of getting his family established in Shanghai.

Dr. Parker, for his part, soon wrote the CES in behalf of Hudson, more fully informing the committee of the extreme deprivations that he had experienced since arriving in China. To the committee's credit, it voted to increase Hudson's salary to sixty pounds per quarter, three times his original salary of four hundred dollars a year, but still less than that of other missionaries in the area.

First Evangelistic Journeys

In recent months Hudson Taylor and other missionaries had regularly ventured out to the towns and villages within a fifteen-mile radius of Shanghai to preach and distribute Christian literature. On Saturday, December 16, 1854, Hudson and Joseph Edkins set out on a weeklong journey in which they hoped to carry the gospel one hundred miles inland.

They hired a large houseboat and set sail down the Huangpu River for Sungkiang. There, on Sunday morning, they made their way to a Buddhist temple where Edkins preached to a large crowd and Hudson passed out Scriptures and tracts. A number of Buddhist priests with shaved heads and yellow robes listened intently as the missionaries shared.

After they were done, the priests gave them an invitation: "Stay and rest a while in our monastery. We would especially like you to visit the holy man who lives here."

Their curiosity piqued, Hudson and Edkins followed the priests into the recesses of the temple and up to a wall with a single opening just large enough for a man's hand to pass through. The priests, smiling politely, pointed to the narrow slot and said, "Look in there. You will see the holy man."

First Edkins, then Hudson peered through the small opening. As their eyes adjusted to the darkness, they were able to make out the form of a man sitting silent and motionless in a chamber that had no doors or windows. To their horror they realized that he had willingly allowed himself to be walled off from the rest of the world. He was bricked in with no means of escape. His only contact with the outside world was via the small slot through which a little food, water, and light passed.

By this means he hoped to cut himself off from the impurities of the world and to achieve complete holiness, thus gaining salvation for his soul. So he sat, day after day and year after year, unwashed and unkempt, seeing and hearing little, talking with no one.

Moved with compassion for this pathetically deceived individual, Edkins spoke to him in a dialect that he could understand about being made holy in God's sight through faith in Jesus Christ. The two missionaries prayed earnestly, then and afterward, that the gospel message heard under those circumstances for the first time might bring light and salvation to the monk's soul.

Wherever Hudson and Edkins went on that journey they magnetized huge crowds of people. Most of the natives in the cities, towns, and villages they visited had never seen Europeans with their curious clothes and haircuts. They had heard wild tales about such barbaric white devils, so many were fearful of them. Still, most people desired the opportunity to observe them, to hear what they had to say, and to read their literature.

At the ancient city of Kashing they sailed to a picturesque island in the middle of a lake on the south side of town. Soon a number of boats were ferrying people from the city to the island so that they could see the foreigners. When a large crowd had gathered, Edkins preached a gospel message. Afterward, Hudson had a long talk with some of the people who flocked around him for books.

In order to avoid having anyone trampled or pushed into the water by the press of the crowd, the missionaries got into their boat and pulled out a bit from the shore. The natives immediately followed them in their boats, and soon they were surrounded in the middle of the lake. As quickly as one boatload of people was supplied with Christian literature, another would move in to take its place. They were kept busy in this way, without any break, throughout the day until evening.

Two months later, toward the end of February 1855, Hudson, Alexander Wylie, and John Burdon set out on foot for a week of itinerating in the inland region southwest of Shanghai. The first Sunday morning away, they climbed a high hill, intending to sing hymns and read Scripture together at a deserted pagoda. Looking to the north, they saw the smoke from an immense fire and realized immediately that Shanghai must be in flames.

Concerned for their family members and friends, they hastened back toward the city. Soon they encountered a few of the many rebel soldiers who, realizing their defeat was imminent, had set Shanghai on fire and fled. The soldiers pleaded with the missionaries to protect them, but they were powerless to do so. Moments later imperial forces arrived, captured the rebels and beheaded them on the spot in the sight of Hudson and his companions.

When the missionaries arrived in Shanghai they had to turn their faces from sights of horror on every hand. The south gate had been blown up, and the city was a heap of smoking ruins. Headless, naked bodies of old men, women, and children lay in streets and courtyards throughout the city. Imperial forces and Shanghai's citizens had wreaked vengeance on the rebel soldiers, their families, and anyone who had collaborated with them.

They were thankful that the European settlement had been spared attack. The imperialists were so jubilant over their defeat of the Triad Rebels that they paid little attention to the foreigners.

"Shanghai is now in peace," Hudson wrote on March 4, a full year after his arrival in China, "but it is like the peace of death. Two thousand people at the very least have perished, and the tortures some of the victims have undergone cannot have been exceeded by the worst barbarities of the inquisition. The city is little more than a mass of ruins, and many of the wretched objects who have survived are piteous to behold."

The missionaries did all they could to help the people of Shanghai start rebuilding their lives after this terrible ordeal. Peace having been restored to the region, Hudson was also anxious to take advantage of the opportunity to further spread the gospel. In April, he and John Burdon traveled by boat up the Yangtze estuary toward the large, populous island of Tsung-ming. Sixty miles long and fifteen miles wide, the island was home to over a million people. Although only thirty miles from Shanghai, Tsungming had never before been evangelized by Protestant missionaries.

They spent several days in the island's chief city, which was also named Tsungming. Burdon preached in four large temples. In the temple of the city-god, Hudson examined patients in a side room while his companion passed out literature and preached in the open courtyard.

When Burdon's voice gave out, it was Hudson's turn to preach. Not being as tall as Burdon, he looked around for some sort of platform from which he could better be seen and heard. The only such object was a very large bronze incense vase. Hudson climbed up on it, without causing any apparent offense to the temple authorities who were present, and preached at the top of his voice to the crowd of a thousand. The people listened attentively. He was encouraged to hear one person after another call out as he preached, "Not wrong, not wrong!" The Chinese customarily used that expression when something that was said met with their approval.

After leaving Tsungming, the missionaries continued up the Yangtze to the large city of Tungchow. Their native guides strongly discouraged them from going there, as the town was known for its unruly mobs that might well treat foreigners roughly. Believing, however, that the Lord would have them to take the gospel to that yet unevangelized city, they committed themselves to His care and set out by wheelbarrow across the seven miles that separated Tungchow from the river.

A short while later a respectable gentleman approached them. "Honorable sirs," he stated soberly, "I must earnestly warn you against proceeding. If you do so, you will find to your sorrow what the Tungchow militia is like." The missionaries thanked him for his concern but remained determined to carry out what they believed to be God's will in this situation.

At that point Hudson's wheelbarrow man refused to go any farther because of the danger. However, it was not difficult to enlist another in his place. Continuing on, Hudson and Burdon encouraged each other with relevant promises from Scripture and verses from hymns. As they approached the city, the prayer of the early Christians in the book of Acts when they first encountered persecution came to Hudson's mind: "And now, Lord, behold their threatenings: and grant unto thy servants, that with all boldness they may speak thy word" (Acts 4:29).

Upon reaching the western outskirts of Tungchow, the missionaries instructed their wheelbarrow men where to wait for them. Then, after another prayer for protection, they picked up their bags of books and headed toward the west gate of the city which stood in the distance.

At first they were unmolested. They thought it curious to hear the people murmuring to one another a new description of them as they passed: "Black devils!" Later they concluded that this had been because of their dark clothes.

As they passed several soldiers who made no move to stop them, Hudson commented to Burdon: "These are the men about whom we have heard so much. They seem willing to receive us quietly enough."

But that illusion was brought to an abrupt end moments later when a tall, powerful man, made fierce by partial intoxication, suddenly approached from behind and seized John Burdon by the shoulders. The missionary tried unsuccessfully to shake him off. Hudson, a couple of steps ahead of Burdon at the time, turned to see what was wrong.

Immediately they were surrounded by a dozen of the drunken man's companions, who began rushing them toward the city. They were hustled along at such a rapid pace that they could hardly keep up. Hudson's bag soon began to feel very heavy in his hand, and he was not able to switch it to the other hand for some relief.

Repeatedly the missionaries insisted, "We demand to be taken before the chief magistrate!"

Their assailants heaped insulting epithets upon them and threatened, "We know where to take you and what to do with you!"

The fierce ringleader let go of Burdon and began torment-ing Hudson. Not being as tall or strong as Burdon, Hudson was less able to resist him. Repeatedly the man pummeled Hudson about, nearly knocking him down. At other times he alternately seized Hudson by the hair, grasped him so tightly by the collar that he nearly choked him, and roughly grabbed his arms and shoulders, leaving them bruised.

Incredibly, even as they were being rushed along, Burdon attempted to give away a few of the books he was carrying under his arm, not knowing whether they would have another oppor-tunity to do so. This further enraged the large soldier, who then ordered that handcuffs be brought. Fortunately there were none available. This threat, however, convinced the missionaries that the wisest course of action was to submit quietly and go along with their captors.

A quarrel broke out among the soldiers regarding what to do with them. "We need to take them to the yamen," stated the moderate members of the group, referring to the local magis-trate's office.

"No!" argued more extreme individuals. "We should kill them at once!"

At one point the two missionaries were jostled together. "Take heart, brother," Hudson stated to his companion. "Remember, the apostles rejoiced that they were counted *worthy* to suffer for the cause of Christ."

Hudson managed to get his hand into a pocket and produced the large red identification card that verified he was a foreigner. After that they were treated with more civility. Up to that point, say what they might, they had been unable to convince the sol-diers that they were foreigners, despite the fact that they were both dressed in English clothing. Apparently they had been mistaken for rebel spies.

"I insist that this card be given to the chief official of the city and that we be taken to his office at once," Hudson stated firmly.

They were hurried through countless streets till they arrived at the residence of a mandarin. Hudson, drenched with perspiration and his throat parched, leaned exhausted against the wall. "Might we have chairs on which to rest?" he inquired.

"You will have to wait until the mandarin is able to see you," he was told.

"Please, then, may we at least have some tea to drink?" he further requested.

"You will just have to wait!" came the terse reply.

A large crowd had gathered around the doorway where they were standing. John Burdon, summoning his strength and courage, took advantage of the opportunity by lifting his voice and sharing the good news about Christ with the onlookers.

The mandarin, who proved to be a lower ranking official, kept them waiting a long time, then decided to send them on to one of his superiors in another part of town. Faced with the prospect of again being roughly escorted through the crowded streets, the missionaries were emboldened to assert: "We positively refuse to move a single step further under these unjust conditions. We insist that chairs be brought and that we be transported in a humane manner."

After considerable hesitation and discussion on the part of the soldiers, this request was granted. As they were carried along, they overheard some in the crowd saying, "They do not look like bad men." The facial expressions of other spectators seemed to betray pity for them.

They were taken to a residence which Hudson first mistook for a prison, as it was guarded by two sets of massive gates. He felt more at ease when he spotted a tablet with the inscription

"The Father and Mother of the People," the title assumed by civil magistrates.

Their identification cards were sent in, and a short while later they were ushered into the presence of the city's chief mandarin. As they came before him, some of the Chinese fell on their knees and bowed with their faces to the ground. One of those escorting the missionaries motioned for them to do the same, but they declined.

This high-ranking official had previously served in Shanghai and understood the importance of treating foreigners courteously. He greeted them respectfully, then invited them into a more private inner apartment.

Hudson explained the purpose of their visit and requested permission to give him copies of their books. Handing the official some gospel tracts as well as a volume that included the entire New Testament and Genesis through Ruth of the Old Testament, he explained what they were and provided a brief summary of their Christian teaching. The magistrate listened attentively, then ordered refreshments to be brought and partook of them with the missionaries.

After a lengthy visit, Burdon queried: "If it please you, sir, might we have permission to see something of your fine city and to distribute among your citizens the books we have brought with us before we return to our boat?"

"It would be our honor to have you do so," the mandarin consented.

Hudson broached another matter: "Sir, as we entered your city earlier today we were treated most disrespectfully. We did not attach much importance to that fact because we realize that the rough soldiery knew no better. However, we have no desire to see the experience repeated. Would you be so kind as to give orders that we are not to be further molested?"

The mandarin readily agreed to this request as well. Accompanying the missionaries to the door of his yamen, he sent several "runners" with them to make sure there would be no further trouble.

Hudson and Burdon distributed their books quickly, then visited the city's Confucian temple. Afterward they were escorted out of town in quite a dignified fashion. As they were carried through the congested streets, they were amused to see a novel use that the runners made of their long braided pigtails, employing them as whips to clear a path so that their honorable guests could pass.

The missionaries returned to the river, accompanied for over half the distance by one of the chief magistrate's attendants. When they arrived back at their boat early that evening, they sincerely thanked God for the gracious protection and aid that He had given them. The next day they returned to Shanghai.

10

Some Radical Changes

In June of 1855, Hudson Taylor, William Parker, and John Burdon traveled south to Ningpo, another of China's primary port cities. There they enjoyed several days of much needed relaxation.

They had to cut their visit short, however, when an urgent summons came for John Burdon, informing him that his son had suddenly become gravely ill. Hudson accompanied Burdon in hurrying back to Shanghai. A couple of weeks later, for the second time in less than a year, he needed to console his friend when the beloved family member died.

Hudson and Dr. Parker were greatly impressed by the missionary community they visited in Ningpo. Nearly a dozen missionaries from various English and American societies worked together harmoniously, carrying out a fruitful ministry which was obviously experiencing the Lord's blessing.

The one aspect of an effective ministry that the Ningpo missionaries lacked was an established hospital work. Not long after Dr. Parker returned to Shanghai, he received a unanimous, formal invitation from the missionaries and European merchants in Ningpo to become their community surgeon. After prayerful consideration, he accepted that invitation and began making plans to move late in August.

On August 6 Hudson received notice that he would need to vacate the residence where he had been staying on the LMS compound by the end of September. The LMS needed the premises for some of its new missionaries who were scheduled to arrive then.

Although he had been invited to do so, Hudson did not believe that God was directing him to move to Ningpo with the Parkers. Instead, he was contemplating quite a different course of action. For months he had been considering the possibility of once again living right among the Chinese, only this time adopting their native dress and other amoral aspects of indigenous culture.

He desired to do this in order to lessen cultural barriers to the dissemination of the gospel and to show his high regard for the native culture of those he was trying to reach. He began a diligent search for a residence in a Chinese neighborhood in Shanghai, but nearly three weeks of concentrated effort yielded nothing.

Hudson had agreed to accompany the Parkers part of the way on their journey to Ningpo. He decided to undertake this trip in native garb. As he returned to Shanghai he would do some itinerating in towns along the way. This would provide him with an initial idea of how well his plan was going to work.

The evening before they were to leave, Hudson went down to hire a junk to take them part of the way to Ningpo. As he was on his way, a man approached him and asked, "Are you still looking for a house in the Chinese city? If so, I think I know of a new one near the south gate. The owner has run short of money and hardly knows how to complete the work. If the house suits you, no deposit will be required. In all probability it can be had for an advance of six months' rent."

Feeling as if he were in a dream, Hudson followed the man to a compact but perfectly new and clean house. It had two rooms upstairs and two down with a fifth for the servants across the courtyard. The house was just what Hudson had been looking for, and he was able to lease it for half a year for the moderate sum of ten pounds.

Late that same evening he hired a barber to shave his head. A single shock of hair on the back of his head was preserved to be grown into a queue. This remaining hair was dyed black, and the next morning it was plaited to a temporary queue of proper length.

That morning he also dressed in Chinese clothing for the first time, adopting the attire of a native teacher. He put on thick socks which were made of calico and which contained no elastic. His satin shoes had flat bottoms and curled up at the front, squeezing his toes uncomfortably. The breeches, which were two feet too wide around the waist, he folded in front and kept in place with a strong girdle. The billowy legs of these trousers fell to just below the knees, and he tucked them into his socks, securing them there with colored garters.

A white jacket with wide sleeves took the place of a shirt. Over all that went a richly colored, heavy silk gown with broad sleeves which reached a full foot past his fingertips. At that time of the year no cap was worn, which caused Hudson's freshly bared head great discomfort in the intense sunlight.

He must have caused quite a stir when he made his first appearance to the Parkers that morning. Dr. Parker looked him over and remarked good-naturedly of the voluminous breeches, "You could store a fortnight's provisions in those!"

As Hudson returned to Shanghai after escorting the Parkers part way to Ningpo, he entered a town and made his way, unnoticed, up a crowded street. The local citizens had no idea that a foreigner was among them until he began speaking to them and distributing literature. They then asked his servants where he came from, and the news spread rapidly.

At first he was not treated as respectfully as he would have been had he been dressed as a foreigner. But that immediately changed when he began to offer medical treatment to the people. Women and children seemed more willing to come to him for treatment than they had before.

Hudson also noticed throughout his return trip that he attracted far fewer troublemakers by not dressing like a foreigner. If he needed to pass through a crowd quickly without causing a stir, he was able to do so. On the whole he concluded that adopting native dress would greatly promote his evangelistic endeavors to China's interior.

Back in Shanghai he soon learned that his fellow Europeans did not approve of the step he had taken across cultural lines. Many merchants and government officials reacted to him with undisguised contempt. More difficult to bear was the obvious disapproval of his missionary associates.

That October, Hudson and two Christian natives sailed to Tsungming Island where he and John Burdon had earlier ministered. The townspeople in the first location where he stopped encouraged him to take up residence there. Within two days they made arrangements for him to rent a six-room house where he could carry out his evangelistic and medical work.

The city's native doctors and druggists, however, quickly became upset over the business he was drawing away from them with his superior and gratis medical treatment, and vehemently protested his presence in their town. The chief magistrate issued a writ against him and all those associated with him in the rental of the house. Hudson's Chinese associates were threatened with a beating of between three hundred and three thousand blows each if they failed to give a "satisfactory" accounting to the mandarin!

Late in November, Hudson received a summons to appear before the British consul in Shanghai, Rutherford Alcock, who was investigating the situation. The consul listened to his case with interest, but then said, "I need to remind you that our country's treaty with China only allows you, as a British subject, to take up residence in one of the five port cities designated in the agreement. If you attempt to settle elsewhere, you render yourself liable to a fine of five hundred dollars. You must return to Tsungming at once, give up your house there and remove your belongings to Shanghai."

Reluctantly, Hudson complied. Shortly after returning to Shanghai, he met William Burns, the first British Presbyterian ever to have gone to China. An effective evangelist, his was a household name in Scotland where, in 1839, a revival had occurred under his powerful preaching. After doing evangelistic work in Ireland and Canada, Burns came to China in 1847. Only recently had he arrived in Shanghai.

Seventeen years older than Hudson, Burns' hair was turning gray, but he still possessed all his youthful evangelistic zeal. The two men began to spend considerable time together and soon discovered that they were kindred spirits. Before long they decided to launch out on an itineration of the inland region southwest of Shanghai. Leaving the coastal city in mid-December, they traveled in separate boats, each missionary having his own Chinese helpers and a considerable supply of Christian literature.

They made their way to Nanxun, just south of Tai Hu ("Great Lake"). There they stayed for eighteen days, preaching and doing personal evangelistic work in the open air as well as at temples, schools, tea shops, and their own boats.

While there, they learned of an immoral play that was being performed in the fields just outside town. Going to investigate, they found a large campsite in which were thousands of people. Prostitution and gambling were being flaunted.

Burns did not hesitate to mount the stage and stop the lewd play, which was in progress when they arrived. "What you are doing is very wrong," he challenged actors and audience alike. "This type of behavior will lead you to hell."

Sponsors of the event had the two missionaries led away firmly, though not roughly. But a more respectable element in Nanxun asked them to make another attempt to put a stop to the wicked proceedings.

The next day they returned, and this time it was Hudson who took to the stage. He commanded the actors to stop and the people to listen. When men started to move forward to stop him, Burns ordered them to sit down.

"Pity your own souls," Hudson pleaded with the actors. "Don't be the bait to allure others to eternal judgment."

Before long he was pulled from the stage, but again was not treated roughly. When he was released, he made his way to a different part of the crowd and stood on a stool, calling out, "What you see all around you is wrong. Is not what I'm saying true?" Many had to agree that it was.

Burns posed another question to the pleasure seekers: "Would you like your own daughters to be in the state of these women?" When he heard people in the crowd repeating his question and answering that they would not, he further queried, "Then why buy other men's daughters for immoral purposes?"

In the end, the missionaries were unable to stop the sinful activities, but doubtless they dissuaded some from participating in them. They next traveled to Wuchen, meaning Black Town, a busy market town with a reputation for lawlessness which served as a haven for salt smugglers.

Things started off well enough there, with ample opportunities to preach and distribute literature. But on the third day, as Hudson was preparing to eat lunch in his boat, a horrific battering of the vessel's roof commenced and soon a hole was broken through it. He immediately went out the back of the boat, where he spotted four or five men taking large chunks of frozen earth from a nearby field and heaving them onto the boat.

His protests were to no avail, and before long the heavy clods, weighing ten or fifteen pounds apiece, had caved in a considerable portion of the roof and covered the boat's inner contents with dirt. Finally, one of their Christian Chinese helpers managed to get ashore and distracted the assailants away from the boat with the offer of some gospel tracts.

As it turned out, the leaders in this attack were not local residents but salt smugglers who had become incensed when their unreasonable demands for more free books from the missionaries had not been granted. When Hudson and Burns returned to the town that afternoon they found a populace that sympathized with them and disapproved of what the trouble-makers had done.

A couple of evenings later they went to the tea shop where they had been meeting with people, thinking that some individuals would likely want to converse with them about spiritual matters. But on that occasion they found no serious inquirers, so Burns suggested they leave earlier than usual.

As they returned to their boats they met one of their boat-men who, without any word of explanation, blew out the candle of their lantern. They relighted it, but to their great surprise he removed the candle and threw it into the canal.

When they demanded an explanation for his peculiar behavior, he responded in an intense whisper: "Please do not continue to speak. Some bad men are seeking to destroy the boats, which we have moved away to another location in order to avoid them."

He led them to the boats, which they boarded. A few minutes later one of their Chinese assistants, Sung, who had also gone to look for them, returned and located their vessels. After the boatmen pushed out into the river, the missionaries were given a fuller explanation.

"A man claiming to be the constable came to the boats in your absence," divulged Sung. "He carried a written demand for ten dollars and a quantity of opium. He said that there were more than fifty salt smugglers waiting for your reply in a nearby tea shop. If you gave them what they wanted, they would leave you in peace. But if not, they would come immediately and destroy your boats.

"I told the man that you could not comply with their demand since you are not engaged in trade but only in preaching and book distribution. I said that you don't have a speck of opium and that your money is nearly all expended, but he would not believe me and promised that there would be trouble.

"I went to search for you while the boatmen moved the boats, but I couldn't find you. Just now, as I repassed the place where your boats had been moored, I saw a dozen or more men among the trees along the riverbank. They were inquiring where your boats had gone to, but no one knew. As I sought to pass unnoticed, they asked me if I knew where your boats were, and I was glad that I could honestly say I did not. Thankfully, they did not recognize me as one of your companions."

The two vessels moved a short distance down the river, but since it was unsafe to travel at night in that region, they found another spot along the bank to moor. Calling together their Christian helpers and the boatmen, the missionaries read Psalm 91 and earnestly implored the Lord to provide them with that sort of divine protection through the night.

The next day brought a torrential rain that not only kept them confined to their boats but also prevented those who had threatened them from searching for them. Early the following morning they were able to set out for Shanghai.

Further Providential Guidance

Hudson and William Burns intended to stay in Shanghai only a few days before returning with a fresh stock of literature and operating supplies to the region where they had just been ministering. Again, however, God redirected their steps.

One weeknight they attended a prayer meeting at Dr. Medhurst's residence, where they met a Christian captain whose ship had just arrived from Swatow. Captain Bowers was deeply burdened over the crying spiritual needs he had witnessed in that coastal city, six hundred miles south of Shanghai. British merchants living on Double Island, just five miles from Swatow, made their fortunes selling opium and engaging in the coolie trade, which was essentially slave trafficking. Not a single missionary ministered there.

"If merchants and traders of all nationalities can live there," Captain Bowers pressed Hudson and Burns after the meeting, "why should not ministers of the gospel?" He then added soberly, "But the missionary who would pioneer his way amid such darkness must not be afraid to cast in his lot with the off-scourings of Chinese society."

Even as the captain spoke, Hudson sensed God calling him to go to minister in Swatow. But he returned to his boat that evening feeling very unsettled. He could not bear the thought of leaving William Burns, who had become a beloved spiritual father to him. For days he resisted the Spirit's prompting, telling himself that it simply could not be God's will that they should separate.

A few nights later Hudson went with Burns to dinner at the home of Robert Lowrie of the American Presbyterian Mission. After they ate, Mrs. Lowrie played and sang a song titled "The Missionary Call." Although Hudson had never before heard the song, it greatly affected him. Before the song was finished he felt like his heart would break. Still he silently spoke to the Lord one of the verses as a prayer:

> And I will go!
> I may no longer doubt to give up friends, and idle hopes,
> And every tie that binds my heart
> Henceforth, then, it matters not, if storm or sunshine be my
> earthly lot, bitter or sweet my cup;
> I only pray, God, make me holy,
> And my spirit nerve for the stern hour of strife.

When they left the Lowries, Hudson asked Burns to come to the little house near the south gate that still served as his headquarters. There he could contain himself no longer, but broke down in tears.

"Oh, my cherished brother," he explained when he was again able to speak, "God has been leading me to go to minister in

Swatow. But I am afraid I have been very rebellious in resisting His call. That is because I was unwilling to leave you, my dear friend, in order to go to that new sphere of labor. But tonight I have surrendered to the Lord and said I will go."

As Burns listened, a look of surprise and pleasure rather than of pain crept across his face. "Hudson," he revealed, "I had determined that this very night I would tell you that I have heard the Lord's call to Swatow. My one regret has been the prospect of severing the happy, holy fellowship which we have enjoyed together."

The next morning they went together to tell Captain Bowers of their mutual leading from the Lord. He was overjoyed and offered both of them free passage on his ship which would be returning to Swatow in a few days. They sailed from Shanghai on March 6, 1856.

When they reached their destination, the missionaries were unwilling to settle among their ungodly fellow countrymen on Double Island, but instead immediately began searching for a place to stay among the Chinese in Swatow. After two days of fruitless investigation, they had a "chance" meeting with a Cantonese merchant whom William Burns addressed in his native dialect.

The man was so pleased at meeting a foreigner who spoke his own language that he befriended them and took a personal interest in helping them locate housing. As it turned out, the merchant was a relative of the highest official in Swatow. With his connections, he was able to find a one-room apartment above an incense shop for them to rent.

The apartment was barely adequate, but as it was the only accommodations they could find, they sought to make the best of it. They hung sheets to divide the apartment into three rooms, a bedroom for each plus a shared study. Their residence was entered by a ladder which projected up through an opening in the floor from the incense shop below. Throughout the summer the apartment was "oven-like" with the roof tiles that served as their ceiling becoming so hot that they could not rest a hand on them.

Before Captain Bowers sailed for Singapore he came to pay them a visit in their new residence. Taken aback by the seeming inadequacy of their accommodations, he remarked to the older missionary, "Surely, Mr. Burns, you might find a better place to live in."

Burns laughed and stated truthfully, "I am more content in the midst of this people than I would be at home surrounded with every comfort. Besides, our total rental expenses here amount to only ten dollars a month."

"Mr. Burns," the captain exclaimed, "that would not even keep me in cigars!"

The local natives, automatically associating them with the degraded European merchants who were involved in the trafficking of opium and coolies, viewed the missionaries with hatred, suspicion, and contempt. Each time they went out among the people they were laughed at and insulted. The epithets most commonly hissed out at them were "foreign devil," "foreign dog," and "foreign pig."

In the outlying towns and villages where they regularly ventured to preach the gospel they frequently encountered danger. The people often described the whole region as being "without emperor, without ruler, and without law." The towns were all walled, and each contained ten thousand to twenty thousand people of the same clan and surname. Not infrequently one town and clan was at war with the inhabitants of a neighboring city. So for the missionaries to be kindly received in one place sometimes became a source of danger in the next.

While ministering in one small town they discovered that the local citizens had captured a wealthy man from another clan and had demanded a large ransom for his release. When he refused to pay it they proceeded to smash his anklebones, one at a time, with a club until they succeeded in extorting the money.

"There was nothing but God's protection," Hudson later testified, "to prevent our being treated in the same way. In circumstances such as these the preserving care of our God was often manifested."

After they had lived in Swatow about three months, the city's chief mandarin became ill, and the native doctors were unable to cure him. He had heard of some townspeople having received beneficial medical treatment from Hudson, so sought his help. Under his care the magistrate soon recovered.

He was so pleased and grateful that he strongly encouraged Hudson to establish a hospital and dispensary in Swatow. He even assisted in the search for suitable premises for such a purpose. With his helpful influence the missionaries were soon able to lease the entire building where they had been renting their one-room apartment.

In July Hudson returned to Shanghai to pick up medical supplies and equipment that he had left in storage on the LMS compound. These he intended to bring back to Swatow for use in establishing an expanded medical work. Upon arrival in Shanghai, however, he was greatly dismayed to learn that a recent fire had destroyed all his medicines and many of his medical instruments.

As medicines were extremely expensive in Shanghai, he decided to visit Dr. Parker in Ningpo, hoping to purchase medical supplies from him at a more reasonable rate. He took with him his few remaining possessions, which included a bed, two watches, a camera, a few surgical instruments, a concertina, and some costly books on the Chinese language. Intending to make the journey as much of a mission tour as possible, he also brought a generous stock of Christian literature.

Progress by boat down the Grand Canal toward Ningpo was excessively slow on that occasion. The surrounding countryside was experiencing a drought, and much of the river's water had been drained off to irrigate the nearby rice fields.

Because of the low water levels, boats were not traveling past Shihmenwan, so Hudson hired two coolies to carry his belongings and, along with his servant, set out on foot for the next town. But before noon, the coolies, heavy opium smokers, complained of exhaustion and quit, while the servant said that he desired to stop and visit a friend in a town along the way. Hudson protested, stating that he needed to reach Haining by nightfall. Haining was on the coast of Hangchow Bay, and from there he could catch a boat to Ningpo.

Instructing his servant to hire new coolies and to meet him in the next town, Hudson walked on ahead of them to Changwan. There, throughout the afternoon, he waited in vain for their arrival. Feeling a bit annoyed and concerned, he began asking local residents whether they had seen his servant and belongings.

"Your things have gone on before you," one man responded to Hudson's inquiry. "For I was sitting in a tea shop when a coolie came in, took a cup of tea, and set off for Haining in a great hurry. He said that the bamboo box and bed he carried, just such as you describe yours to have been, were from Shih-menwan, and he had to take them to Haining tonight, where he was to be paid at the rate of ten cash a pound."

As it was getting dark by then, Hudson was forced to spend the night there in an inn. The only items on the inn's menu that evening were cold rice (which also turned out to be burned) and snakes fried in lamp oil! His bed that night, in a room shared with ten other lodgers, consisted of some boards that had been placed on top of two stools.

The next day he made his way to Haining, arriving late in the afternoon. There he was told that a servant with belongings that fit his description had been seen earlier, headed for the Great East Gate where retailers traded wares with seagoing junks. Further inquiries in that business district yielded no additional information.

Again Hudson was left with no other option than to spend the night in the city. But none of the local innkeepers were willing to rent him a room. Finally, after midnight, he settled down on the stone steps of a temple, hoping to get some sleep there.

He had not been there long when he saw the shadowy figure of a beggar, who no doubt intended to rob him, stealthily approaching. The man, thinking that Hudson was asleep, began to feel about him gently.

"What do you want?" Hudson asked in a calm but firm tone.

Startled, the beggar left. But a while later he returned, this time with a companion. Again supposing him to be asleep, one of the men started to probe under his head for his money.

"What are you doing?" Hudson demanded.

The beggars, sitting down at his feet, replied, "Like you, we're going to pass the night here."

"Well, please move to the other end of the steps and leave this side for me. There's plenty of room for you to sleep elsewhere." The would-be thieves, however, refused to move, so he raised up and sat with his back against the wall.

"You had better lie down and sleep," the men coaxed. "If you don't, you'll be unable to walk tomorrow. Don't be afraid. We shall not leave you, and we'll make sure no one hurts you."

"Listen to me," said Hudson sternly. "I do not want your protection; I don't need it. I am not a Chinese; I do not worship your senseless, helpless idols. I worship God; He is my Father; I trust in Him. I know full well what you are and what your intentions are. I shall keep my eye on you and shall not sleep."

Having heard that, one of the beggars went away, but soon came back with a third man. Hudson felt very uneasy but silently lifted to God a prayer for protection. As the night passed slowly, he became very drowsy. To keep himself awake and to cheer his mind, he sang several hymns, recited aloud some Scripture passages, and prayed in English, all to the great annoyance of his unwanted companions. Shortly before dawn the beggars left him for good, and he was able to get a little sleep.

That morning he walked back to Changwan where he was able to have a good dinner and napped for a few hours. Awaking much refreshed, he set off for the next town, the one where he had parted from his servant and belongings two days earlier.

Along the way he started reflecting on God's constant goodness to him and remembered that he had failed to pray for appropriate lodgings while in Haining the previous night. He also felt convicted that he had become so anxious about his few material possessions while being relatively unconcerned about the many precious souls all around him. He began to pray for himself, for friends in England, and for his fellow missionaries. "Sweet tears of mingled joy and sorrow flowed freely," he later reported, "the road was almost forgotten, and before I was aware of it I had reached my destination."

That evening he did pray about an adequate place to sleep and was invited to stay on a passenger boat that was left idle in the dry riverbed. The next morning he continued on to Shihmenwan, where he hoped to catch a boat back to Shanghai. He had just enough cash in hand to buy a boat ticket and to pay for the other provisions of the return trip.

But when he arrived at the boat office he was distressed to discover that no passenger boat would leave that day and perhaps none the next. The daily mail boat had already left as well. His only hope that day was to hire a private boat to take him to Kashing, the next large city along the river, but all attempts at doing so proved futile.

Just then he spotted a mail boat, which apparently had been unexpectedly detained, headed in the direction of Kashing. With renewed hope, he ran along the canal after it for about a mile.

"Are you going to Kashing?" he called out after overtaking the vessel.

"No," came back the terse response.

"Are you going in that direction?"

"No."

"Will you give me a passage as far as you do go that way?"

"No," was the blunt reply once again.

Completely dispirited and exhausted, Hudson slumped down on the grass and fainted. As he regained consciousness several minutes later, he heard voices and realized that he was the subject of discussion.

"He speaks pure Shanghai dialect," one person said. From their speech he knew that the people who were talking about him were also from Shanghai. Sitting up, he saw that they were on a large passenger boat which was stranded in the shallow water on the far side of the canal. A few minutes later they sent a smaller boat to pick him up and bring him to their junk.

The boat people were very kind, providing him with some tea and food. When he took off his shoes and socks to relieve his blistered feet, they brought him hot water in which to soak them. They hailed passing boats in his behalf, but none of them would take him as a passenger.

Later that day, the junk's captain spotted a mail boat coming from downriver, headed toward Shanghai. He drew it to Hudson's attention, but the missionary divulged that he did not have adequate funds to pay the more expensive passage that the mail boat would require to transport him. The captain hailed the boat anyway and learned that it was going to a town about nine miles from Shanghai. From there the boatmen would carry the mail overland to the coastal city.

"This gentleman is a foreigner from Shanghai who has been robbed and no longer has the means of returning," the captain explained to the boatmen. "If you will take him with you as far as you go, and then engage a sedan chair to carry him the rest of the way, he will pay you in Shanghai. You see that my boat is now lying aground for want of water and cannot get away. I will stand surety, and if this gentleman does not pay you when you get to Shanghai I will do so on your return."

When the boatmen agreed, Hudson gratefully climbed into their long, narrow craft. He really did not mind the fact that he needed to lie down the whole time he was in the boat, which had very little room inside. He was thankful for the opportunity to rest while speeding toward his destination via China's quickest means of river travel. Two days later, on August 9, he arrived in Shanghai.

As Hudson made further inquiries about his missing servant and personal belongings it became apparent that the man had stolen the possessions and fled. Others strongly encouraged him to have the thief tracked down and imprisoned, but he hesitated to do so. He had prayed much for this man's salvation and had taught him Christ's teachings from the Sermon on the Mount about turning the other cheek rather than resisting evil.

Concluding that the man's soul was worth infinitely more than the possessions that had been stolen, Hudson decided to write him a letter in hopes that his conscience might be moved. Among other things he wrote:

> At first I considered handing over the matter to the yamen. Had I, you know what the consequences might have been to yourself. But remembering Christ's command to return good for evil I have not done so. You are the one who stands to be the real loser in this affair, not I. I freely forgive you, and beseech you more earnestly than ever to flee from God's wrath to come through repentance and faith in the Lord Jesus Christ.

Shortly after that letter was posted, Hudson received a correspondence from a friend in England. The letter from home, mailed eight or ten weeks before the theft, included a check for forty pounds, the exact worth of his stolen possessions!

Later that month he traveled without further incident to Ningpo. There he was able to purchase medicines from Dr. Parker for the medical clinic that he anticipated establishing in Swatow.

Staying on in Ningpo a few weeks, he assisted Parker with his extensive medical work. During that visit he met John and Mary Jones, the newest missionaries sent out by the Chinese Evangelization Society. A strong friendship began to develop between Hudson and John, and they did some evangelistic work together in the outlying towns and villages.

Early in October Hudson returned to Shanghai. Captain Bowers was there and once again offered him free passage on his ship to Swatow. Then, after his belongings had already been loaded on the ship, a stunning letter arrived from William Burns.

He and two of his Chinese ministry assistants had been arrested and imprisoned for preaching the gospel. Under custody, Burns was taken on a thirty-one-day journey by rivers and canals to Canton where he was turned over to the closest British consul. It would likely be quite some time before he could return to the region from which he had just been ejected. Missionary activities in and around Swatow would have to be suspended for the time being.

Hudson realized that his path was once again being providentially redirected. After prayerful consideration, he concluded that the Lord would have him move to Ningpo to assist his CES colleagues in evangelistic and medical work.

12

Difficulties in Ningpo

Hudson set out promptly for Ningpo. Accompanying him was an intelligent young Chinese man who had traveled abroad to various countries including England. There he began to go by the name Peter. He had accompanied William Parker from England when he first came to China. Recently Peter had written to Dr. Parker and had received permission from the physician to come and work for him in Ningpo.

Peter was not a Christian, and Hudson was burdened for him. On the first night of their journey to Ningpo, Hudson earnestly conversed with him about his need for salvation. Peter listened attentively, and was even moved to tears, but still made no definite commitment to Christ.

The next day Hudson was in his cabin when suddenly he was startled by a loud splash and a cry for help. Immediately jumping up on deck, he found the other men aboard the boat looking helplessly back toward the spot where Peter had fallen in and disappeared under the water.

A strong wind was rapidly propelling the junk up the river and away from Peter. Hudson quickly let down the sail, then leaped into the water and began searching for the submerged man. Failing to locate him, he spotted a nearby fishing boat with a dragnet that could be used to bring up Peter's body.

"Come!" he called out. "Come and drag over this spot; a man is drowning here!"

"It is not convenient," responded the uncaring fishermen.

"Don't talk of convenience!" Hudson shouted back. "A man is drowning, I tell you!"

"We are busy fishing and cannot come."

"Never mind your fishing," Hudson pleaded. "I will give you more money than many a day's fishing will bring. Only come—come at once!"

"How much money will you give us?" queried the fishermen, showing a glimmer of interest.

"We cannot stop to discuss that now!" the missionary responded, hardly believing what he was hearing. "Come, or it will be too late. I will give you five dollars."

"We won't do it for that," the men bargained callously. "Give us twenty dollars and we will drag."

"I do not possess that much money. But do come quickly and I will give you all I have!" Hudson promised in desperation.

"How much may that be?"

"I don't know exactly. About fourteen dollars."

Finally, but even then slowly, the fishermen paddled over and let down their net. Less than one minute later Peter's lifeless body was brought to the surface. Even as Hudson sought to resuscitate him, the fishermen clamored indignantly that their promised payment was being delayed. He was unable to revive the drowned man.

Hudson later reflected on this tragedy:

To myself this incident was profoundly sad and full of significance, suggesting a far more mournful reality. Were not those
fishermen actually guilty of this poor man's death, in that they
had the means of saving him at hand, if they would but have
used them? Assuredly they were guilty.

And yet, let us pause ere we pronounce judgment against
them, lest a greater than Nathan answer, "Thou art the man."
Is it so hardhearted, so wicked a thing to neglect to save the
body? Of how much sorer punishment, then, is he worthy who
leaves the soul to perish, and Cain-like says, "Am I my brother's
keeper?" The Lord Jesus commands, commands me, commands
you, "into *all* the world, and preach the gospel to *every* creature."
Shall we say to Him, "No, it is not convenient"?

Hudson arrived in Ningpo late in October of 1856. This large
city of four hundred thousand inhabitants was surrounded by
five miles of walls. Hudson took up residence in the barn-like
attic of a building that William Parker had leased on Bridge
Street in the southern section of the city. Dr. Parker used the
main floor of the building as a daytime dispensary and school
for boys as well as a chapel where gospel preaching services
were held in the evening.

The attic where Hudson lived had a tiled roof that repelled
the rain, but as winter snows came, some managed to blow in
through various crannies and crevices. One morning Hudson
awoke and traced his initials in the thin layer of snow that had
collected on his blanket while he slept! Eventually he divided
the spacious attic into four or five smaller rooms by erecting
wooden walls and installing ceilings.

Near the center of the city, about a mile from where
Hudson settled, a forceful Englishwoman named Mary Ann

Aldersey operated a Protestant girls' school, the first of its kind in China. Miss Aldersey had been one of the first missionaries to arrive in Ningpo, having commenced her tireless labors there in 1843. She was so influential that some local natives believed that, just as England was ruled by a woman, Queen Victoria, so Miss Aldersey had been delegated to be the head of the British community in Ningpo. Some supposed that even the British consul took orders from her.

When the tremors of an earthquake alarmed the citizens of Ningpo, they credited it to Miss Aldersey's magical powers. She had been seen mounting the city wall early that morning and opening a bottle of strong spirits which had proceeded to shake the pillars of the earth. She actually took a 5 a.m. walk along the wall each morning throughout the year, in the wintertime having a Chinese servant walk ahead of her with a lamp. The bottle she carried contained only smelling salts that she regularly used to relieve headaches.

Miss Aldersey was assisted in the work of her mission school by two attractive young ladies, Burella and Maria Dyer. Their parents had served as missionaries in China when they were young girls, so they grew up speaking fluent Chinese. Both their parents died before the girls became teenagers, and they were subsequently brought up under the guardianship of an uncle in London, spending most of their time at a Quaker boarding school in Darlington in northern England. Late in their teens, having received some training as teachers, they returned to China in response to an appeal that Miss Aldersey had made for assistance with her girls' school.

The Parkers, the Joneses, and Hudson were sometimes invited to dinner at Miss Aldersey's home. Miss Aldersey generally disapproved of Hudson, viewing him as something of a renegade beacuse of his lack of connection with a denomination and, especially, his decision to wear Chinese clothing and a native hairstyle. Nineteen-year-old Maria Dyer, on the other hand, found herself strongly attracted to the earnest young man. She told no one about this, but made it a matter of private prayer instead.

In the closing months of 1856 hostilities developed between China and England over trade issues as Britain continued to insist that its importing of opium into China be legalized. After one incident involving the arrest of some opium smugglers, the British navy bombarded Canton and temporarily took possession of its yamen. When the British troops withdrew, the viceroy of Canton vowed to take revenge and put a price on every foreigner's head.

Wherever this news spread to Cantonese people throughout China, foreigners came under grave danger. This became the case in Ningpo, where a considerable Cantonese population resided. Although Hudson and the other missionaries actually spoke out against Britain's actions in connection with the opium trade and the attack on Canton, that was not widely known, so they were hated and detested along with all other foreigners.

Early in January 1857 the Cantonese of Ningpo devised a scheme to destroy all the foreigners in the city. It was commonly known that many of the foreigners habitually met for worship on Sunday evening at one of the missionary homes. They would simply attack and kill all those present at such a gathering and afterward execute any foreigners who happened to be absent.

The Cantonese had no difficulty in obtaining permission from Ningpo's chief civil magistrate to carry out this action.

Generally speaking, the Cantonese were feared and disliked in many parts of China because of their ravenous, lawless behavior which was often carried out in a clandestine manner. On this occasion, however, the magistrate was only too willing to allow them to carry out their planned treachery against the despised and resented foreigners.

A local resident who was aware of this conspiracy had a friend who was a servant for one of the missionaries. Fearing for the friend's life, the local warned him of the imminent danger and urged him to leave the employ of the foreigners at once. The servant, in turn, told his employer, and the missionaries were thus made aware of the perilous situation. They immediately gathered at one of their homes for prayer, beseeching God to protect them.

Even as they prayed, the Lord providentially directed a lesser public official, the superintendent of customs, to pay a visit to the chief magistrate. He suggested the folly of permitting such a massacre, pointing out: "It would surely rouse the foreigners in other places to come with armed forces to avenge the deaths of their countrymen. They will raze the city to the ground."

"When the foreigners come for that purpose," the magistrate responded, "I shall deny all knowledge of or complicity in the plot. That will direct their vengeance against the Cantonese, who will in their turn be destroyed. And thus," he concluded triumphantly, "we shall get rid of both Cantonese and foreigners by one stroke of policy."

The customs official, however, held his ground, predicting that all such attempts at evasion would be futile. In the end, the chief magistrate was convinced and sent word to the Cantonese, withdrawing his permission and forbidding them to carry out the attack. It was several weeks before the missionaries learned about this interview and that it had taken place at the very time they were collectively praying for God's deliverance.

Because of the threatening circumstances that lingered, the Ningpo missionaries decided to send their wives and children to Shanghai. The securest British settlement was there and, in the event of war, that might be the only port held by foreigners. Because of his extensive connections and experience in Shanghai, Hudson was asked to help escort the missionary family members to that city and to remain there with them indefinitely.

Miss Aldersey opted to remain at her school in Ningpo, and the Dyer sisters, although encouraged to go to Shanghai, chose to stay and assist her. Hudson, for his part, was inwardly reluctant to leave Ningpo, having started to become romantically attracted to Maria Dyer. When the missionary party departed for Shanghai, Hudson and Maria were unaware of the feelings each had begun to privately cherish for the other.

That winter thousands of famine refugees from Nanking had poured into Shanghai. They took shelter from the cold wherever they could find it, including in run-down, abandoned buildings and even tombs. Unable to find work, they were reduced to begging. Unfortunately, hundreds died of starvation, disease, and exposure. Hudson helped with regular food distribution efforts to the starving refugees and sought to minister to their spiritual needs as well.

As he labored in Shanghai, Maria Dyer was very much in his thoughts. Eventually his feelings for Maria slipped out, quite unintentionally, to his good friends the Joneses, who had come with him to Shanghai. They heartily encouraged him to inform her of his true thoughts and to entrust the outcome to God.

On March 21 Hudson wrote Maria a letter in which he expressed his feelings about her and asked whether he might be allowed to become better acquainted with her with a view toward marriage. When she received the correspondence in early April, she was thrilled and immediately divulged the delightful news to her sister. Together they went to inform Miss Aldersey, hoping that she would approve of the relationship.

Instead she responded indignantly, "Mr Taylor! That young, poor, unconnected Nobody. How dare he presume to think of such a thing. Of course the proposal must be refused at once, and that finally!"

When Maria sought to express the mutual affection she had for Hudson, Miss Aldersey became more upset, exclaiming: "Innocent child, you must be saved without delay from such folly. I want you to write to Mr. Taylor immediately, not only to close this whole affair, but also to request most decidedly that it might never be reopened. I insist on reading the letter before it is mailed."

Bewildered and heartbroken, Maria sat down to her difficult task a week later after much prayer. She wrote a masterful letter with carefully chosen wording that might satisfy Miss Aldersey while at the same time hinting to Hudson of her true feelings in the whole affair. A portion of her letter stated:

I have made the subject of your letter a matter of earnest prayer to God, and have desired, I think sincerely, only to know His will, and to act in accordance with it. And although it gives me no pleasure to cause you pain, I must answer your letter as appears to me to be according to God's direction. And it certainly appears to be my duty [note she did not say "desire"] to decline your proposals. But think not, dear sir, that I do so carelessly, and without appreciating the kind feelings which you express towards me. And I have too great a respect for those feelings (although my duty requires me entirely to discourage them) to expose you and the subject of your letter to ridicule.

It was right that I should acquaint Miss Aldersey and my sister with the matter. Mrs. Bausum, the new head-mistress at our school, is the only other person who knows anything about it, as far as I am aware. And it is my desire that no one else except my own immediate relations, and those to whom you have thought or may think proper to acquaint with the matter, should ever know anything about it.

I regard you, dear sir, as a brother in Jesus, and hope ever to bear towards you those feelings which disciples are commanded to bear to one another. But ask me not for more. I request you not to refer to the subject again as I should be obliged to return the same answer. You will perceive by the tone of my letter that I have not lightly sent you a refusal.

Maria later testified of her own thoughts after Miss Aldersey had given her approval to the letter and it had been posted: "I felt that I could not wish one way or the other. I could only leave the matter in God's hands, praying Him to do what He saw best." She took comfort in the fact that absolutely nothing that was the Lord's will would be too difficult for Him to accomplish. If He desired them to be engaged and married, He would bring it about.

When Hudson received Maria's reply in early May, he read it repeatedly and carefully. He perceived a degree of ambiguity in her response and suspected that Miss Alder-sey's involvement might have had something to do with that.

Privately he continued to make the whole affair a matter of earnest, ongoing prayer.

At the end of that same month, one week after his twenty-fifth birthday and more than three years in China, Hudson felt compelled to make a decision that, from a human perspective, would further jeopardize his opportunities to court Maria. For months he had been protesting to the committee of the Chinese Evangelization Society its heavy indebtedness of over a thousand pounds and its policy of paying the quarterly salaries of its missionaries with borrowed monies. When it became clear that the CES was making no serious efforts at rectifying this situation, Hudson felt obligated to resign his position with the society for reasons of conscience.

He later explained his personal convictions on this matter:

> To me it seemed that the teaching of God's Word was unmistakably clear: "Owe no man anything." To borrow money implied, to my mind, a contradiction of Scripture—a confession that God had withheld some good thing, and a determination to get for ourselves what He had not given. Could that which was wrong for one Christian to do be right for an association of Christians? Or could any amount of precedents make a wrong course justifiable? If the Word taught me anything, it taught me to have no connection with debt. I could not think that God was poor, that He was short of resources, or unwilling to supply any want of whatever work was really His. It seemed to me that if there were lack of funds to carry on work, then to that degree, in that special development, or at that time, it could not be the work of God.

John Jones joined Hudson in resigning from the CES for the same reason. They were gratified to learn that, while the society would not be changing its policies regarding indebtedness, several of the committee members agreed with their convictions and the resulting decision to resign. They were also deeply thankful that their separation from the CES took place without the slightest disruption of friendly feeling on either side.

Joined in Marriage and Ministry

Hudson and the Joneses were now independent missionaries. Without a mission society to support them, they planned to trust God to supply their needs through acquaintances back home who were aware of their situation. Hudson was willing to be a tentmaker if necessary while continuing to devote as much time and attention as possible to missionary endeavor.

In June of 1857 they were able to return to Ningpo. For several months Hudson lived with the Joneses in a home that they rented. William Parker was willing to lease the entire premises on Bridge Street, where Hudson had formerly resided, to him and the Joneses. This provided them with an adequate facility where they could carry on their active evangelistic ministry in a busy part of town.

Before long, Mary Jones invited Maria Dyer to join her in doing evangelistic work among the Chinese women and to visit with her in her own home. Miss Aldersey, not at all pleased that

Maria might encounter Hudson at the Joneses' house, angrily confronted Mary at a ladies' prayer meeting:

"I feel I have good reason to be indignant," the overbearing matriarch exclaimed. "Miss Dyer belongs to a different social circle from that of Mr. Taylor. She has a small but reliable income of her own, unlike Mr. Taylor, who so far as I can see has no regular source of income with which to propose supporting a wife. Maria is educated, gifted, attractive, and has no lack of suitors who are far more eligible in my eyes.

"I think it unpardonable that this person has presumed upon her youth and inexperience. It's still more so that he has returned to Ningpo after it has been made plain that he is not wanted here. Now you must promise me that you will do nothing more to forward Mr. Taylor's suit and that hereafter he will never be allowed to see or speak to Miss Dyer in your house."

Mary, being careful to keep her own provoked temper in check, responded: "While I cannot commit myself as far as that, Miss Aldersey, I will refrain from throwing the couple together. And I'm completely confident that Mr. Taylor would not seek to take advantage of Miss Dyer's visits by attempting to see her alone. At the same time, I feel compelled to say, Miss Aldersey, that it is a very serious matter for you to tamper with the affections of two young people."

One afternoon in the middle of July, that same ladies' prayer group met at Mary's home. As the meeting drew to a close, a torrential downpour commenced. Most of the women were able to leave, but two of the missionaries, Maria Dyer and Mrs. Bausum, were detained as they waited for coolies to come and carry them in sedans through the flooded streets.

As supper time neared, Hudson and John Jones arrived home from the Bridge Street chapel where they had been ministering. When they were told by a servant that Maria and

Mrs. Bausum were still there, Hudson immediately wondered whether God had providentially arranged an opportunity for them to meet.

"Go into my study," John recommended, "and I will see if an interview can be arranged."

When John suggested the meeting to Maria, she responded: "It is what I of all things wish." In keeping with the conservative conventions of the day, she added, "I should like Mrs. Bausum to be present."

Hudson was thrilled with the opportunity, for the first time since returning to Ningpo over a month earlier, to look into the lovely face of Maria and converse directly with her. Despite the fact that a third party heard everything that was said, he couldn't help but fully and freely express his deep affection for her. Then he asked, "Might I write to your guardian, Mr. Tarn, seeking his permission to cultivate a permanent relationship with you?"

"Yes, you have my consent," Maria readily assented. Then she further revealed: "Mr. Taylor, please know that you are just as dear to me as I apparently have become to you. I was compelled by another to reject your earlier proposals, but I have suffered great personal distress as a result."

He lost no time in writing to her uncle in London. Then there was nothing to do but patiently, prayerfully await the response by return mail in about four months. So as not to antagonize Miss Aldersey, the couple agreed not to visit or even write each other until a response was received from the guardian.

Maria felt obliged to inform Miss Aldersey of Hudson's correspondence with her uncle. Thoroughly incensed, the matriarch fired off a letter of her own to Mr. Tarn in which she aired all her criticisms of Hudson. She represented him as being "called by no one, connected with no one, and recognized by no one as a minister of the gospel." She even went so far as to declare that he was "fanatical, undependable, diseased in body and mind, and totally worthless."

Meanwhile Hudson sought to carry on faithfully in his ministry efforts. One evening a local cotton merchant named Nyi Yongfa was walking down Bridge Street when his attention was arrested by a ringing bell. Inquiring, he learned that foreign teachers were about to discourse on religious matters in their "Jesus Hall." Being a devout Buddhist with unsettled questions about the penalties due his own sins and the unknown journey of the soul after death, he entered the chapel.

Hudson's text that night was John 3:14–16. He shared how that forgiveness of sins and eternal life could be gained through looking to God's Son, Jesus Christ, who had died on the cross to pay the penalty for the world's transgressions. Nyi was astounded to hear in this message the answers to his plaguing spiritual questions. The Spirit of God opened his heart so that right then and there he embraced the truth he heard and received Christ as his personal Savior.

When the missionary finished speaking, Nyi stood up, looked around the audience, and testified: "I have long sought the Truth, as did my father before me, but without finding it. I have traveled far and near, but have never discovered it. In Confucianism, Buddhism, Taoism, I have found no rest; but I do find rest in what we have heard tonight. Henceforth I am a believer in Jesus."

Shortly after Nyi's conversion, there was a meeting of the Buddhist society that he had formerly led. Having resigned from the society, he requested permission to attend the meeting, accompanied by Hudson, in order to share the reasons for his sudden change of faith. Hudson listened with delight as the new convert proclaimed the gospel with clarity and power. As a result of this testimony, another member of the sect was led to saving faith in Christ.

A few days later Nyi surprised Hudson by asking, "How long have you had the Glad Tidings in England?"

The missionary felt a degree of shame as he divulged, "Several hundreds of years."

"What?" exclaimed the man, "Several hundreds of years? Is it possible that you have known about Jesus so long, and only now have come to tell us?" Sadness registered on his face and in his voice as he continued: "My father sought the truth for more than twenty years and died without finding it. Oh, why did you not come sooner?"

That fall Hudson and the Joneses began providing a free daily breakfast for many of the poor people to whom they ministered. Soon sixty to eighty people who otherwise would have had very little to eat each day were being fed a good breakfast and attending the chapel service that followed. More than once this new ministry drained the missionaries' financial resources nearly dry, but the Lord always faithfully provided as they continued to depend on Him.

At the end of November, Hudson and Maria received the anxiously awaited letters from the Tarns. The guardians had made careful inquiry of George Pearse of the Chinese Evangelization Society as well as others in London who were acquainted with Hudson, and discovered that all had nothing but the highest commendation for the young missionary. In fact, Mr. Tarn had become convinced that Hudson was a missionary of unusual promise.

"I cordially consent to my niece's engagement," he wrote to Hudson. "My only request is that the marriage should be delayed until she comes of age in the new year."

So Hudson was able to formally propose to Maria, and she joyfully accepted. They set the wedding date for January 20, 1858, four days after her twenty-first birthday.

Exactly two weeks before they were married a situation arose that allowed Maria to affirm her willingness to share Hudson's life, even with the full awareness that doing so would sometimes involve financial sacrifice and trials of faith. Weeks earlier, Hudson and the Joneses had invited Maria and Mrs. Bausum to come to their home for dinner on the evening of January 6. But when that morning came they found themselves with virtually no food or money. Their ministry to the poor had exhausted their resources, and mail after mail had come without funds.

A single coin with a square hole in the center, worth only one-twentieth of an English penny, was all the money they had between them. After eating a modest breakfast, they had no other food left for the rest of the day. They urgently implored their heavenly Father to provide the needs of His children, especially reminding Him of their painful circumstance of not having the means to feed their dinner guests that evening.

Holding strictly to their policy of not borrowing money, they decided the only thing they could do was to sell a little used stove that they possessed as scrap iron. They set out with it to a distant foundry, but when they reached the river along the way they were unable to cross. Normally one could walk across the river on a bridge of boats, but such was not the case that day. Not having enough money to take the ferry, they returned home, believing that God must be intending to provide for them in some other way.

Mary Jones and her children had been invited several days earlier to have lunch that day at a friend's house. While they were away, Hudson and John searched the cupboards and found only a small packet of cocoa. Mixing that into some hot water, they drank it and felt somewhat refreshed. Then they again went to prayer about their straitened condition. While they were still on their knees, their servant came to the door and exclaimed, "Oh Teacher, Teacher, here are letters!"

The mail had arrived from England several days before it was expected. Among the letters they found one containing a substantial contribution from their most generous supporter back home, William Berger.

That evening Hudson gave Maria a full account of the day's circumstances and events, then stated soberly: "I cannot hold you to your promise if you would rather draw back. You see how difficult our life may be at times."

"Have you forgotten?" she responded. "I was left an orphan in a far-off land. God has been my Father all these years. And do you think I shall be afraid to trust Him now?"

After the wedding, Hudson and Maria made their home in the spacious attic he had remodeled in the Bridge Street residence. There they happily shared in joint ministry. Hudson was kept busy preaching, teaching, and dispensing medicine. Maria invested six or seven hours daily teaching in the school they had on the premises.

In June of 1858 the Treaty of Tientsin was signed, ending China's second war with the European powers. That accord opened up ten additional port cities plus the entire Yangtze River region, which stretched hundreds of miles inland. Foreigners were given the right to travel freely under the protection of passports, and Chinese Christians as well as missionaries were promised freedom to exercise their faith without molestation.

A few months later Hudson wrote home:

You will have heard before this all about the new treaty. Many of us long to go inland—oh how we long to go! But there are duties and ties that bind us that none but the Lord can unloose. May He give "gifts" to many of the native Christians, qualifying them for the care of churches already formed, and thus set us free for pioneering work.

Late in August, tragic news was received from Shanghai. Maria's sister, Burella, had moved there earlier in the year after her marriage to Hudson's good friend John Burdon. John wrote the end of August to report that Burella had died suddenly of cholera. She was only twenty-three. Burdon, at age thirty-two, had lost two wives and a child to death since coming to China. Deep sadness returned a short while later when, in October, Maria gave birth prematurely at seven months to an infant who did not survive.

The summer of 1859 brought a return of dangerous anti-foreign sentiment to Ningpo. Many Europeans left the city, but Hudson and Maria felt they could not desert the new Chinese converts who were also in grave danger because of their Christian faith. One day toward the end of July, with Maria ready to have another baby at any time, an angry crowd surged around their mission hall, shouting menacingly: "Beat the foreigner! Kill the foreign devils!"

A few days later, on Sunday, July 31, Maria gave birth to a daughter whom they named Grace Dyer. The following week William Parker persuaded Maria to bring her newborn and stay for a time at his safer hospital compound just outside the city wall.

Stunning tragedy soon came again when, late in August, Mrs. Parker was stricken with cholera and died within hours. Dr. Parker was benumbed with grief and decided that he must take his children home to live with their grandparents in Scotland.

Hudson was asked to take over Parker's responsibilities in running the hospital and dispensary. It was a huge task, with care being given daily to fifty or more inpatients, about half of whom were recovering opium addicts. In addition, a large number of outpatients—more than six hundred by year's end—came to the dispensary for treatment.

The expenses to keep the hospital and dispensary operating were enormous and, as before, Hudson needed to look in faith to God to provide. One morning, after he had been overseeing the medical work for a few weeks, the hospital's cook anxiously informed him, "The very last bag of rice has been opened and is disappearing rapidly."

"Then the Lord's time for helping us must be close at hand," the missionary responded reassuringly.

Before that bag of rice was consumed Hudson received another letter from William Berger, this one containing a check for fifty pounds. Berger wrote:

> A heavy burden has come upon me, the burden of wealth to use for God. My father recently passed away, leaving me a consid-erable increase of fortune. I do not wish to raise my standard of living as I had enough before. The enclosed check is for any immediate needs which you might have. Would you be so kind as to write fully, after praying over the matter, if there are ways in which you can profitably use more?

Great was the rejoicing of Hudson and his little band of faithful Christian workers when he relayed this news to them. They were not bashful about sharing the joyous news with the hospital's unconverted patients as a testimony of the power and love of the one true God of the Christians.

A New Mission Founded

By the early part of 1860, after six years in China, Hudson's strength and health were quickly failing him. It became increasingly difficult for him to carry out the excessive demands that were placed on him in the Ningpo hospital ministry. He and Maria decided that they should return to England for a time of recuperation. Reluctantly, they closed the Ningpo mission hospital and bid farewell to the beloved Bridge Street congregation, which now had more than twenty committed adult members.

Late in June they left Ningpo for Shanghai, and on July 18 sailed for England. They were accompanied by Wang Laedjun, one of the committed young Christians from Ningpo.

Early in the new year, 1861, Hudson received a thorough medical examination in London and was bluntly told by the doctor, "You must never think of returning to China unless you wish to throw your life away."

The young missionary couple, however, had no intention of giving up on their God-given call of service to China. With the help of Wang they set to work on producing a pair of much-needed works in the Ningpo dialect, a more accurate translation of the New Testament and a hymnbook. Frederick Gough, another Ningpo missionary home on furlough, also played a major role in the revision of the testament.

Hudson felt led of the Lord to complete his course of medical studies at the London Hospital. For that reason they settled into a small apartment at No. 1 Beaumont Street, Whitechapel, nearby the hospital. Hudson began dividing his time between medical studies and Bible translation work. That spring, on April 3, they experienced joy at the birth of their first son, whom they named Herbert Hudson.

In July of 1862 Hudson passed his exams and became a member of England's distinguished Royal College of Surgeons (MRCS). Three months later he completed another degree, the Royal College of Surgeons' Licentiate in Midwifery, LM(RCS). On November 23 he attended Maria as she gave birth to their second son, Frederick Howard.

After his medical studies were completed, Hudson devoted large blocks of time each day except Sunday to revising the Ningpo New Testament. Commonly he spent ten or twelve hours per day on that project.

Late in the spring of 1864 Wang returned to China. A few weeks later, on June 24, Hudson and Maria's third son, Samuel, was born. That same summer brought an end to the Taiping Rebellion in China. The war, which had dragged on for sixteen years, led to the deaths of twenty million people from fighting, reprisals, famine, and disease.

With such needy conditions in China, Hudson was anxious to return to the field. The crucial New Testament revision still needed to be completed, however. Furthermore, God had been laying an expanded vision on his heart. On the wall of the study where he did his translation work hung a large map of the vast Chinese empire. As he contemplated the map, he came to be increasingly burdened for the whole of China. He later explained:

> While on the field, the pressure of claims immediately around me was so great that I could not think much of the still greater need farther inland, and could do nothing to meet it. But detained for some years in England, daily viewing the whole country on the large map in my study, I was as near the vast regions of the interior as the smaller districts in which I had personally labored.

As Hudson and Maria's family grew it became necessary for them to seek a larger residence. In October they moved three quarters of a mile farther east, to No. 30 Coborn Street in the more residential neighborhood of Bow. Frederick Gough made this move possible by offering to pay the difference in rent for them.

During that time, Hudson interviewed or corresponded with all of the main English missionary societies about the need to send workers to the eleven unevangelized provinces of inland China. Repeatedly he was told that available funds were not equal to current demands, much less taking on new commitments.

Through the early months of 1865 Hudson sensed the Lord prompting him to establish a mission that would have as its objective the evangelization of the inland regions of China. Knowing the marked challenges, trials, and responsibilities such an undertaking would entail, he hesitated. For weeks he wrestled with the Lord about the decision.

"Suppose the workers are given and go to China," he reasoned with himself. "Trials will come. Their faith may fail. Would they not reproach *you* for bringing them into such a plight? Have you ability to cope with so painful a situation?"

At the same time he could not escape the persistent thought, which seemed burned into his very soul, that one million people each month were dying in China without God. For two or three months he hardly slept more than an hour at a time night or day and feared he might begin to lose his reason. Still he would not give in to the Lord's leading.

Late in June he was invited to spend the weekend at George Pearse's seaside home in Brighton. On Sunday he attended a large Presbyterian church where he heard a stirring message. But he could not bear the sight of a congregation of a thousand Christian people rejoicing in their own security while millions were perishing in China for lack of knowledge. After the church service he wandered along the seashore in great spiritual agony.

Finally he prayed: "Divine Master, I surrender myself to You for this service. All the responsibility as to outcomes and consequences must rest with You. As Your servant it is mine to obey and to follow You. It is Yours to direct, to care for, and to guide me and those who will labor with me.

"God, I ask You for twenty-four fellow workers, two for each of the eleven inland provinces which are without a missionary and two for Mongolia." Opening his Bible, he wrote in the margin above Job 18: "Prayed for 24 willing, skillful laborers, Brighton, June 25/65."

He later related: "The conflict ended, all was joy and peace. I felt as if I could fly up the hill to Mr. Pearse's house. And how I did sleep that night! My dear wife thought Brighton had done wonders for me, and so it had."

Two days later, accompanied by George Pearse, Hudson went to the London and County Bank. There he opened an account under the name of The China Inland Mission (CIM) with an initial deposit of ten pounds, the American equivalent of fifty dollars.

In addition to its unique objective of evangelizing China's inland provinces, the CIM had several other distinguishing features. It was open to workers from various denominational backgrounds and was receptive to candidates with little formal education who clearly had aptitude in evangelism and in learning the Chinese language. The new agency was also much more open to sending single women as missionaries, and did not confine them to the traditional role of schoolteacher.

With regard to finances, no appeals for funds were made. CIM missionaries, who were not guaranteed set salaries, confined their appeals for support to God alone in prayer, looking in faith to Him to supply all their needs. Under no circumstance would the CIM incur debt. "Depend upon it," Hudson often said, "God's work done in God's way will never lack God's supply."

The mission was committed to embracing amoral aspects of indigenous culture as a courtesy to the Chinese. CIM missionaries all consented to wearing Chinese clothing and to worshiping in Eastern- rather than Western-style buildings.

CIM activities in China would be directed by Hudson on the field rather than by a committee in the distant homeland. William Berger agreed to oversee the mission's responsibilities in England. He corresponded with candidates, received and forwarded contributions, sent out suitable workers as funds permitted, and published an *Occasional Paper* which included news from the field as well as audited accounts.

Throughout his extended furlough time in England, Hudson welcomed the opportunity to preach and share his burden for China in churches representing a wide variety of denominations including Anglican, Baptist, Brethren, Methodist, and

Presbyterian. After his decision at Brighton, such opportunities increased dramatically. There was great interest in his new mission and its objectives.

Late that summer Hudson began devoting considerable time to the writing of a small book titled *China's Spiritual Need and Claims*. In the sitting room of their house, Hudson paced back and forth, dictating the volume line by line to Maria, who sat writing at a table.

The work clearly set forth the crying spiritual needs in China. Although mission work had made good progress in the seven coastal provinces of China during recent decades, 185 million people in those regions still had never heard the gospel. An additional 200 million individuals in eleven inland provinces were without a single Christian witness. One million people per year, thirty-three thousand each day, were perishing without Christ.

In the face of that immense need, the book pointed to the only One capable of meeting it, God Himself. Attention was drawn to God's limitless resources, infallible promises, and undying faithfulness. Finally, the booklet delineated the main objective of the newly founded CIM and some of the distinctive principles it would adhere to in order to accomplish that goal.

When the book was completed, William Berger underwrote the expense of having the first edition of three thousand copies printed. These were available just in time for distribution at a prominent Christian convention, the Mildmay Conference, held at the end of October.

Six weeks earlier, Hudson had been able to address several hundred delegates at a similar Bible conference in Perth, Scotland. Through the exposure he gained at these conventions, interest in the CIM mushroomed to extraordinary proportions. Speaking invitations flooded in and requests for literature were so great that *China's Spiritual Need and Claims* had to be reprinted within three weeks.

Applications from potential candidates picked up, so that by year's end nearly thirty individuals had made serious inquiry. Plans were being made and supplies gathered to send out a party of at least ten or twelve people in the near future. Once again the Taylors' house became too small for all these activities, and they were delighted when the opportunity presented itself to rent the premises next door, thus doubling their available accommodations.

Hudson wrote to his mother during that period of overwhelming activity and responsibility:

> The Ningpo New Testament revision is now going on. We have reprinted the pamphlet, and have missionary boxes on the way. I am preparing a magazine for the Mission, furnishing a house completely, setting up two fonts of type for China, teaching four pupils Chinese, receiving applications from candidates, and lecturing or attending meetings continually—one night only excepted for the last month. I am also preparing a New Year's address on China, for use in Sunday schools, and a missionary map of the whole country. Join us in praying for funds and for the right kind of laborers, also that others may be kept back or not accepted, for many are offering.

By January of 1866 demands on him were so great that he needed to turn over the work of revising the Ningpo New Testament entirely to Frederick Gough. Hudson devoted much time to itinerating, speaking of China to Christian groups in various cities in both England and Ireland. Whether addressing large or small gatherings, he faithfully carried out his opportunities to inform people of China's spiritual needs. The results were significant.

The evening he was to speak in Birmingham, for instance, the weather was so stormy that it looked doubtful there could even be a meeting. A torrential rain was falling and Hudson's host noticed that the missionary already looked extremely weary.

"No one will be able to get to the Seven Street Schoolroom on a night like this," the host commented. "It will be taken for granted that the meeting will not be held."

"But was the meeting not announced for tonight?" Hudson asked quietly. "Then I must go, even if there is no one but the doorkeeper."

Go he did, and the Lord worked mightily in the small schoolhouse gathering that evening. Hudson often related afterward that half the tiny audience of eight or ten people at that meeting either became missionaries themselves or dedicated one or more of their children to foreign service, while the other half were from that day on earnest, prayerful supporters of the CIM.

That spring, plans were finalized for a CIM party of eighteen adults and four children to depart for China. The cost of transporting and outfitting such a party was enormous, more than two thousand pounds. But each day, over the noon hour, a prayer meeting was held at the Taylors' home, and in answer to those earnest petitions the funds were fully supplied in timely fashion.

Hudson thought it would be advantageous for the group if accommodations could be found on a ship where the missionaries were the only passengers. This, too, became a matter of fervent prayer at the daily meetings, but by the end of April no such arrangement had come available.

Then on May 2, Hudson spoke at Totteridge in Hertford County just north of London. That important meeting was chaired by wealthy, influential Colonel Puget. The colonel thought it peculiar to have a missionary meeting without a collection. But

understanding that to be Hudson's wish, he had accordingly
announced that no offering would be received. As the meeting
progressed, however, Puget found the presentation unusually
interesting and realized that people would give generously if
only they were presented with the opportunity.

When Hudson had finished speaking, therefore, the chair-
man rose and stated: "Interpreting the feelings of the audience
by my own, I'm going to take it upon myself to alter the decision
about the collection. Many present here have been moved by
the condition of things which Mr. Taylor has represented, and
would go away burdened unless they could express practical
sympathy. Contrary, therefore, to previous announcements,
an opportunity will now be given—"

"Colonel Puget," Hudson interrupted as he stepped before
the assembled guests once again, "if I may be allowed to add
a few words to my earlier remarks." He smiled, but earnest
words flowed from his lips: "My friends, it is my desire that
you do go away from this meeting burdened. Money is not the
chief thing in the Lord's work, especially money easily given,
under the influence of emotion. Much as I appreciate your kind
intention, I would far rather have each of you go home to ask
God very definitely what He would have you do. If it is to give of
your substance, you can send a contribution to our own or any
other missionary society.

"But in view of the appalling facts of heathenism, it might
be much more costly gifts the Lord is seeking—perhaps one
of your sons or daughters or maybe your very own life service.
No amount of money can save a single soul. What is needed
is men and women filled with the Holy Spirit who will give
themselves to the work in China and to the work of prayer at
home. For the support of God-sent missionaries, funds will
never be lacking."

Colonel Puget acquiesced, but that evening at supper he remarked to Hudson, "You made a great mistake, if I may say so. The people were really interested. We might have had a good collection."

The next morning the colonel appeared somewhat late for breakfast, apologizing and explaining that he had not had a good night of rest. After breakfast he invited Hudson into his study where he handed him several contributions that guests at the previous day's meeting had left for the CIM.

As he did, he revealed: "I felt last evening that you were wrong about the collection, but now I see things differently. Lying awake in the night, as I thought of that stream of souls in China, a thousand every hour going out into the dark, I could only cry, 'Lord, what wilt Thou have *me* to do?' I think I have the answer."

He handed the missionary a check for five hundred pounds, adding: "If there had been a collection yesterday I should have given a five-pound note. This check is the result of no small part of the night spent in prayer."

That very morning at the breakfast table Hudson had received a letter from his shipping agents offering the entire accommodations of the *Lammermuir* which was about to sail for China. Returning to London that day, he went straight to the docks, where he found the ship completely suitable for their needs. After signing over Colonel Puget's check as the down payment for their travel fare, he hurried home to share these joyous developments with his family and fellow missionaries.

Progress and Problems

The *Lammermuir*, with its thirty-four-member crew and the CIM party of eighteen adults and the Taylors' four children, set sail on Saturday, May 26, 1866. This was the largest delegation of missionaries sent out to China by any mission society to date.

Throughout the voyage Hudson and Maria met with their fellow missionaries each morning and afternoon to study the Chinese language. Captain Bell gave Hudson permission to lead a weekly Sunday morning worship service in the saloon. Other missionaries, both men and women, met with smaller groups of sailors for Bible reading and prayer at various times throughout the week. The result of these earnest evangelistic efforts, faithfully bathed in prayer, was that a number of the crew professed faith in Christ.

Toward the end of the voyage, the *Lammermuir* encountered a fifteen-day stretch of perilous weather as it navigated through a pair of typhoons off the coast of Taiwan (then named Formosa) and in the East China Sea. By Saturday, September 22, the lifeboats and two sets of bulwarks had washed away and a pair of large sails toward the front of the ship tore loose from their supports. In quick succession two more booms and three masts, including the main mast, gave way.

Conditions on deck were terrifying. Foaming waves washed over both sides of the ship. Massive masts and booms swung about wildly on wire ropes, threatening to crash onto the deck at any moment. Floating timbers and casks banged around the deck. Loose chains clanged and torn sails slapped loudly in the howling winds.

The sailors gave up trying to save the ship. The missionaries gathered in the saloon to pray. Captain Bell, half his face paralyzed by an illness he had been suffering throughout the prolonged storm, entered the saloon and ordered, "Put on your life belts. She can scarcely hold together two hours more." The missionary party began to sing "Rock of Ages."

The captain, looking grim and carrying his club, turned toward the forecastle where the crew huddled in fear and despair. Hudson, who remained calm throughout the ordeal, stepped up to him and said, "Please, sir, don't use force till everything else is tried."

After kissing each of his children, Hudson led the male members of the CIM out onto the deck where they began to secure floating objects. Eventually they coaxed some of the crew into joining them. Laboring in knee-deep water, they succeeded in securing the swinging masts. As they worked away for hours, they periodically ate biscuits with cheese or butter to keep up their strength. Through the next two days both men and women missionaries helped to man the pumps as the storm gradually blew itself out.

When the *Lammermuir* arrived in Shanghai the following Sunday, its badly battered condition attracted considerable attention. The missionaries were doubly grateful for the protection God had given everyone aboard their ship when another vessel, which arrived shortly after the *Lammermuir*, reported that sixteen of its company of twenty-two people had perished in the same storm.

The new missionaries spent a few weeks in Shanghai. They immediately adopted Chinese dress and hairstyles as had been agreed upon before leaving England. That led the Shanghai papers to poke fun at the "pigtail mission."

On Saturday, October 20, they set off for Hangchow, a large city located one hundred miles inland up the Grand Canal. A handful of missionaries already ministered there but, with over a million inhabitants in the city, many more Christian workers were needed. Hudson saw this as a strategic base from which to move farther inland. Quite a stir was made over the six unmarried women in the CIM party who were also headed for Hangchow. Prior to that time, no single female missionaries had served outside the port cities.

In Hangchow they were able to lease a large two-story house with some thirty rooms at No. 1 New Lane. The well-built structure had once been the home of a wealthy mandarin. Having become somewhat dilapidated during the Taiping Rebellion, the house no longer held any interest for merchants or mandarins. But both the size and location of the home, in a quiet neighborhood not far from busy streets and the city wall, made it ideal for the missionaries. There were ample rooms for all the missionaries to sleep upstairs, with single men and women being housed in separate wings, and the downstairs rooms could be used for a chapel, medical dispensary, printing office, guest hall, dining room, and servants' quarters.

In December Hudson did some evangelistic work in the town of Siaoshan, ten miles from Hangchow. It was decided to establish a CIM station there as well. They were able to rent a house in Siaoshan on the condition that the foreigners living there would wear Chinese clothing. Lewis and Eliza Nicol, who had sailed with the CIM party on the *Lammermuir*, were appointed to pioneer that work.

Living in Hangchow at that time was a Church Missionary Society couple named George and Adelaide Moule. The Moules, who were about the same age as Hudson and Maria, strongly disapproved of CIM missionaries wearing Chinese dress. They also objected to the fact that single men and women missionaries were residing in the same house at New Lane.

The Moules invited the Nicols and a few other CIM missionaries to their home for meals and freely aired their disapproval. That had a detrimental effect on a handful of the new missionaries, especially on Lewis Nicol, who began to share with the Moules inaccurate and exaggerated criticisms of CIM operations.

Early in January of 1867 the Nicols moved to Siaoshan. Later that month Lewis Nicol returned to Hangchow to request that a Chinese evangelist be sent to begin work in their new chapel. The missionaries at New Lane were stunned to see Nicol wearing European clothes and to learn that he had been doing so the whole previous week. Nicol's action upset and concerned Hudson, but he decided not to challenge him about the issue immediately. He feared that he might respond inappropriately to Nicol in the heat of the moment.

Tsiu Wenli, a teacher converted under the Taylors' ministry in Ningpo, had come to Hangchow to assist them in their new ministry there. Hudson agreed to let Tsiu accompany Nicol back to Siaoshan. The following Sunday, Tsiu preached in the chapel, and on Monday the two men ventured out into the streets, Nicol wearing his English clothes.

That evening the town magistrate, along with about fifty soldiers and lesser officials, came to the house chapel. The magistrate, who was drunk, refused their offer of tea, would not acknowledge their passports, and insisted on being shown through every room in the house. Then, turning abruptly toward Tsiu, he commanded, "Beat him!"

The Nicols stood by helpless and horrified as Tsiu endured six hundred lashes to his back with rods and another hundred to his face with a strip of leather. After the inhumane beating, the magistrate demanded of Nicol, "Will you leave the house tomorrow?" The missionary nodded and the magistrate left after making a final chilling threat: "If any of you remain tomorrow, you will be beheaded."

Early the next day all the CIM representatives in Siaoshan returned to Hangchow and related this shocking turn of events. Hudson immediately wrote the British consul in Ningpo, detailing for him exactly what had happened in Siaoshan and requesting that official action be taken in their behalf.

He also asked Nicol to assume Chinese dress again. The latter refused, stating, "I will not be bound neck and heel to any man."

"If you persist in wearing English clothes," Hudson sought to explain, "it is likely to prove injurious and possibly dangerous to the mission."

"Then I suppose I had better make my way at once to one of the free ports," threatened Nicol.

"That may indeed prove to be the best course," Hudson agreed simply.

Still he remained patient and cordial toward the younger colleague in the weeks to follow. Nicol, however, continued to wear European clothing and even refused to attend CIM meetings.

Despite these tensions, the Taylors did experience some significant joys during that period of time. February 3, 1867, witnessed the birth of their second daughter, Maria Hudson Taylor. Scores of attentive Chinese attended their Sunday morning worship service each week, and by the end of March there were a dozen new converts desiring to be baptized.

The medical work was also going strong with Hudson seeing over two hundred patients daily. Tsiu spent most of his time talking with the patients about their spiritual needs while they waited to be examined. Hudson generally gave a short evangelistic address each day to those who had come for medical attention.

In March, George Moule wrote Hudson a letter that was both suspicious and accusatory in tone:

> My main objection is that by domiciling in your own house so many unmarried females you are doing that which, if I am not mistaken, would be viewed with mistrust and disapproval even in England; and which among the Chinese gives a reasonable handle to the worst of imputations upon the morality of European Christians.
>
> Living as you do in very confined premises, having some of the restraints of social etiquette relaxed by your relation to these ladies as their physician, and some by the position you have assumed as their spiritual pastor, having them, further, to so large an extent dependent upon you as their only easily accessible friend and adviser of experience in China, since you have removed them from the neighborhood of the bulk of missionary society—you would be more than human if you were not capable of being tempted to lay aside in some measure the reserve with which for their sakes and your own they ought to be treated.

To counter those disparaging intimations, all the ladies of the *Lammermuir* party (except Eliza Nicol and a close friend whom she had influenced) put into writing a testimonial of their own:

Our household arrangements in Hangchow are far more strict, and "the restraint of social etiquette" more rigidly observed than they would be at home; and in Mrs. Taylor, whose presence among us seems to have been ignored, the lady members of our mission have one to whom they can at all times look for sympathy and counsel. We have no sympathy with any movements made to assail Mr. Taylor's character, which has been, throughout our intercourse with him, that of a gentleman, a Christian, and preeminently a Christian missionary.

Unfortunately the Moules and Nicols remained critical of Hudson and the CIM for months to come. They even wrote to acquaintances in England, broadcasting their disapproval to them. Naturally, Hudson and Maria were deeply distressed when they began to learn of this months later through letters received from William Berger. Thankfully, Berger and Hudson's other close acquaintances in England remained unswerving in their faith in him despite the unjust criticisms being leveled against him.

It would be more than a year and a half before Hudson would reach the painful conclusion that he must dismiss Lewis Nicol from the CIM. In his letter to Nicol he stated: "I do not dismiss you because of your denominational views, nor yet for your preference for the English costume, nor indeed on any other ground in whole or in part than that of habitual and deliberate falsehood."

Most of the CIM staff was relieved when their leader took this action and marveled that he had patiently borne with the divisive individual for such a long time. As Hudson feared might happen, however, three single lady missionaries who had always sympathized with the Nicols resigned from the CIM. The entire affair grieved Hudson deeply.

That August of 1867, when the summer heat became unbearable in the city, the CIM delegation in Hangchow spent a few days vacationing at a lovely spot in the hills six miles from town. There they could sit in the shade of giant trees, listen to the music of mountain streams, and look out over a panorama of hills, canals, rivers, and the Hangchow Bay.

Their accommodations for that holiday were in a pair of buildings not far from a temple where idols were still worshiped. The first day they were there, eight-year-old Grace Taylor spotted a man making an idol.

"Oh, Papa," she exclaimed earnestly, "he doesn't know about Jesus, or he would never do that! Won't you tell him?"

Taking her by the hand, Hudson walked over and shared the gospel with the idol maker as Grace listened with intense interest. After leaving the man, they found a shady place to sit and rest. Grace was still deeply concerned for the native and seemed relieved when her father suggested they pray for him. Hudson later recalled:

> We sang a hymn, and then I said, "Will you pray first?" She did so, and never had I heard such a prayer. Her heart was full, and she was talking to God on the man's behalf. The dear child went on and on, pleading that God would have mercy upon the poor Chinese and would strengthen her father to preach to them. I never was so moved by any prayer. My heart was bowed before God. Words fail me to describe it.

Just a couple of days later, Grace suddenly developed a headache and a high fever, then quickly became incoherent. Diagnosing her as having meningitis, Hudson realized that there was little chance she would survive and spent most of the day in tears. He wrote to William Berger on August 15:

> Beloved brother, I know not how to write or how to refrain. I seem to be writing, almost, from the inner chamber of the

King of kings. Surely this is holy ground. I am trying to pen a few lines by the couch on which my darling little Gracie lies dying. Dear brother, our flesh and our heart fail, but God is the strength of our heart and our portion forever.

It was no vain nor unintelligent act when, knowing this land, its people and climate, I laid my wife and children, with myself, on the altar for this service. And He whom we are and have been seeking to serve—though so unworthily, with much of weakness and failure, yet in simplicity and godly sincerity, and not without some measure of success—He has not left us now.

Grace developed pneumonia and died the evening of Friday, August 23. Hudson wrote to his mother out of the depth of his grief the following month:

Except when diverted from it by the duties and necessities of our position, our torn hearts will revert to the one subject, and I know not how to write to you of any other. Our dear little Gracie! How we miss her sweet voice in the morning, one of the first sounds to greet us when we woke—and through the day and at eventide. As I take the walks I used to take with her tripping at my side, the thought comes anew like a throb of agony, "Is it possible that I shall never more feel the pressure of that little hand, never more hear the sweet prattle of those dear lips, never more see the sparkle of those bright eyes?" And yet she is not *lost*. I would not have her back again. She is far holier, far happier than she could ever have been here.

Pray for us. At times I seem almost overwhelmed with the internal and external trials connected with our work. But He has said, "I will never leave thee nor forsake thee," and "My strength is made perfect in weakness." So be it.

16

"Save Life! Save Life!"

By the spring of 1868 Hudson was eager to press farther inland and establish new missionary stations there. The work at Hangchow was coming along nicely. Wang Laedjun, the man who had accompanied the Taylors on their extended furlough to England, arrived in Hangchow in the latter part of 1867 to assist in that developing ministry. Hudson gladly appointed Wang as the pastor of Ningpo's growing Chinese congregation which, by early 1868, had fifty baptized believers.

The CIM had rented a second home on New Lane. No. 1 now housed most of the married couples and the single women while John McCarthy and his wife resided in No. 2 along with the single men. It was decided that the McCarthys and Jennie Faulding, a bright, young single missionary who had experienced exceptional success in her evangelistic work with Chinese women, would take up the oversight of the ongoing mission work in Hangchow.

On April 10, 1868, the Taylors, a handful of other CIM missionaries, and several Chinese Christians left Hangchow and slowly made their way up the Grand Canal on a houseboat. They spent three weeks in Soochow, assisting members of their mission who had recently established a work there.

Continuing on in a northwesterly direction into formerly unreached territory, they crossed the Yangtze River and progressed twelve miles farther up the Grand Canal to Yangchow, a city of 360,000 inhabitants without a single gospel witness. There, in mid-June, they rented some rooms from a local innkeeper. A month later they were able to lease a large house in a long lane shared by several other Chinese homes.

At first the citizens of Yangchow seemed receptive enough toward them. So many people came to wander through their home and inspect their belongings, in fact, that they had to insist that only women from mandarin families could venture upstairs where the bedrooms were.

It was not long, however, before members of the city's literati began to stir up trouble. These scholars, anxious to preserve ancient Chinese traditions as well as the time-honored teachings of Buddhism, Taoism, and Confucianism, began circulating dark rumors about the missionaries in hopes of forcing them to leave Yangchow. Handbills were distributed which accused foreigners, including the missionaries, of scooping out the eyes of the dying, cutting open pregnant women to make medicine, and eating children in their hospitals.

Before long the missionaries noticed a marked change in the attitudes of the townspeople toward them. Friendly visitors to their home were replaced by a menacing mob just outside the courtyard gate. The house had to be barricaded on Saturday, August 15, when reports of a likely riot were received. Hudson wrote to Prefect Sun, the city's top official, asking him to put a stop to the illegal, hostile treatment, but received an evasive response.

On Sunday and again on Tuesday the rabble attempted unsuccessfully to break into the house. A horrid poster was circulated, threatening that the house and all its occupants (now numbering thirteen missionaries, including their children, and nineteen Chinese Christians) would be burned by midweek. God providentially protected the small band of believers from that fate by sending a heavy rain that dispersed their antagonists for a time.

When Hudson again sent a correspondence to Prefect Sun, he excused his failure to stop those who were stirring up the trouble by stating, "As persons who get up this kind of report and placard generally do it in the dark and without either name or surname, it is not easy for me in a short time to lay hold of them."

The following Saturday, August 22, 1868, two American diplomats happened to visit Yangchow to see its temples and pagodas. They were readily visible as they toured the city in their foreign clothes. Immediately after their departure a wild rumor swept through the city that twenty-four children were suddenly missing.

Late that afternoon a massive, restless crowd of eight to ten thousand people gathered in the long street that led to the CIM house. Some individuals brandished knives, clubs, and spears. Others began throwing chunks of brick against the house.

Hudson dispatched yet another message to the prefect but received no response. He and fellow missionary George Duncan decided that they would need to attempt to reach the prefect's yamen themselves. After pausing to pray for God's protection of those they were leaving and of themselves as they went out among the mob, they slipped through a neighbor's house, and away from the hostile crowd.

Before long, however, they were spotted and began to be chased. Hudson knew an alternative route through some fields and, as it was getting dark, they were able to avoid their assailants for a time. But eventually they had to go through the main street where rocks and bricks were hurled at them.

The gatekeepers at the yamen, alarmed by the yells of the oncoming mob, were shutting but had not yet barred the gates just as Hudson and Duncan arrived. The mob rushed against the missionaries, and the press of the crowd burst open the gates. "Had the gates been barred," Hudson stated later, "I am convinced that they would not have been opened for us, and we should have been torn to pieces by the enraged mob."

The missionaries were catapulted headlong into the yamen's courtyard. Quickly picking themselves up, they rushed into the judgment hall, shouting, "Kiu-ming! Kiu-ming! (Save life! Save life!)" That was the sole plea that a Chinese mandarin was obligated to respond to at any hour of the day or night.

They were taken to the chief secretary's office where they had to wait for forty-five minutes before they could speak to the prefect. The whole time they waited they could hear the shouts of the crowd back at the CIM house more than a mile away. For all they knew the mob might be trying to destroy not only the house, but also the lives of those trapped inside it.

Finally they were ushered into the presence of Prefect Sun. He began to probe them with suspicious questions: "What have you really done with the babies? Is it true that you bought them? What is the cause of all this rioting?"

Hudson, unable to restrain himself, burst forth in response to the latter query: "Your Excellency, the real cause of all the trouble is your own neglect in not taking measures when the matter was small and manageable. And I must now request that you take steps immediately to repress the riot and save any of our loved ones who might still be alive. After that you can make whatever inquiries you wish. Otherwise I cannot answer for the result."

The prefect responded reflectively: "Ah, very true, very true! First quiet the people and then inquire. Sit still, and I will go to see what can be done." Just before he left the room he added, "Remain here. My only chance of accomplishing any good depends on your keeping out of sight."

After Hudson and Duncan had left for the yamen, Maria gathered the women and children in her bedroom upstairs to pray while the men sought to guard the doors downstairs. Eventually, however, the mob succeeded in breaking into the house. Missionary William Rudland hastened upstairs to warn those who were still gathered in prayer.

Then they heard Henry Reid, another missionary, calling from the courtyard below: "All of you come down at once if you can. They're setting the house on fire. You'll have to drop from the roof."

Rudland climbed out the window onto the projecting roof and began to assist women and children in dropping the twelve feet to the stone-paved courtyard below. Just then a tall, bare-chested man entered Maria's room.

"You see we are all women and children," she confronted him firmly. "Aren't you ashamed to molest us?"

The man made no reply but began to frisk them. He took Maria's wedding ring, the brooch from another missionary's hair, and the small purse that yet another had hidden under her dress. After that he began searching the drawers and boxes.

Rudland managed to assist one of the three remaining lady missionaries in escaping from the roof to the courtyard below. But then the tall assailant attacked him, grabbing him by the hair and dragging him down onto the roof. He sought to take Rudland's watch, but the missionary managed to throw it into the dark courtyard. Rudland hoped the man might leave them to go search for the watch, but instead the enraged looter picked up a brick and raised his arm to smash it down on the mission-ary's head.

Courageously, Maria put out her arm to stop the blow. When he turned to hit her instead, she looked directly at him and demanded, "Would you strike a defenseless woman?"

Startled, the man dropped the brick. Climbing to the edge of the roof, he shouted to the rioters below, "Come up, come up!" Then he left the missionaries, reentering the house through the window to resume his looting.

A fire had been ignited in the courtyard to cut off their escape route, but Reid managed to move the heap of burning objects to one side. "There's not a moment to lose," he called up to them. "You must jump. I'll catch you."

Maria, who was six months' pregnant, had no choice but to follow his instructions. Reid helped to break her fall, but she still landed on her side with her right leg twisted under-neath her.

Struggling to her feet, she turned in time to see mission-ary Emily Blatchley leap from the roof. Maria watched in horror as a thrown brick hit Reid on the side of the face just as Emily jumped. Momentarily blinded and nearly knocked unconscious by the blow, Reid was unable to catch Emily, and she fell heavily on her back. Her hair, worn in the Chinese style, helped to cushion the blow to the back of her head. Amazingly, she was able to get up and even assisted Reid in doing the same.

At last Rudland was able to drop from the roof to the ground. The battered party was able to make its way undetected to the kindly neighbor's house next door. Mercifully, they were taken to an inner room of the home where they could remain hidden. Reid lay groaning on the floor. Emily was unable to move her left arm which, it was later discovered, had a compound fracture of the elbow. Maria was bleeding from a cut she had sustained, but her sprained leg caused her even greater pain.

One of her children asked, "Mama, where shall we sleep tonight as they have burned up our bed?"

"God will give us somewhere to sleep," she calmly assured the youngster.

Hudson and Duncan were kept in a "torture of suspense" for two long hours at the yamen. Finally the prefect returned, accompanied by the governor of the city's military forces.

"All is now quiet," Prefect Sun reported to the missionaries. "The military governor and his soldiers went to the scene of the disturbance. They seized several of those who were plundering the premises and will have them punished."

The prefect then gave orders for chairs to be brought and for the missionaries to be escorted back to their home. "All the foreigners at the house were killed!" they heard people saying to each other as they passed through the streets. They could only cry out to God for His support, should this report prove to be true, and hope that it was not.

A scene of utter chaos greeted their eyes when they reached the house. A pile of half burned reeds revealed one of the spots where people had attempted to set the house on fire. One wall had collapsed and its debris was scattered about. Strewn all through the house were broken boxes and pieces of furniture, papers and letters, as well as the smoldering remains of valuable books.

Their family members and friends were nowhere to be seen, so they began an anxious search for them. Relief and gratitude swept over them when they discovered their loved ones were still alive and safely concealed in the neighbor's home. They soon learned that it was neighbors, too, who had put out the fires in their house.

The missionaries were able to return to their home shortly after midnight. Every room in the house had been ransacked except Emily's, which was left untouched. Amazingly, that was the room where the mission's most important papers and most of its money were kept. There was no other explanation for why that room had been inadvertently passed over by the looters than God's providential hand of protection.

Some soldiers had been left to guard the premises, so the missionaries were able to get a little sleep that night. Incredibly, when the guard left early the next morning, people began entering the house again in hopes of further plundering the foreigners' goods. Hudson had to rush back to the yamen again to request protection. Once more the other Christians gathered upstairs in Maria's bedroom to pray for God's deliverance. They were greatly relieved when the mandarin and his soldiers returned to disperse the malicious crowd that had begun to gather again.

That afternoon the missionaries, carried in sedan chairs by coolies, were escorted safely out of the city by a contingent of soldiers. As they left, some of the people were heard to say derisively, "Come again! Come again!"

"Yes," thought Maria, "God will bring us back again, little as you expect it."

The CIM party settled temporarily in Chinkiang on the other side of the Yangtze River. When the British authorities were informed about the hazardous developments in Yangchow they were deeply concerned and unwilling to let them pass unchecked. On September 8 the British Consul General, M. H. Medhurst, left Shanghai for Yangchow on a small steamer, escorted by a detachment of marines. They were also accompanied by the French consul and a French frigate.

Medhurst and his soldiers marched conspicuously through the main streets of Yangchow to Prefect Sun's yamen. The consul general insisted that the prefect come with him to Nanking to give an account in person to the imperial viceroy as to why he had not responded more quickly to the CIM crisis. Intimidated by the display of foreign strength, Prefect Sun agreed to do so, under the condition that he could travel to Nanking in his own boat rather than as a prisoner.

The British and French officials and soldiers proceeded on to Nanking where they were received respectfully by Viceroy Zeng Guofan. Medhurst laid out a series of demands that the Chinese officials at first seemed inclined to grant. But then the commander of Medhurst's military retinue became seriously ill and had to be rushed back to Shanghai in the gunboat. With Medhurst's show of force removed, he was no longer treated respectfully by the Chinese, nor were his demands granted. He was forced to return to Shanghai to begin carrying out a long and difficult series of negotiations.

In November, Sir Rutherford Alcock sent five gunboats upriver to Nanking to reinforce Medhurst's efforts to get Chinese officials to honor their treaty responsibilities of protecting the rights of foreigners who resided in their cities. The threat of imminent military confrontation with the Europeans succeeded, and the Chinese finally agreed to Medhurst's demands.

As a result, an elaborate public ceremony was held on November 18 to formally reinstate the CIM missionaries in their Yangchow home. Medhurst and Hudson were led through Yangchow's streets in a solemn procession made up of scholars and mandarins. The two ringleaders of the August riot had been arrested. A pair of heralds at the head of the procession announced to the onlookers, "People—take care not to hurt the foreigners, or to call them 'foreign devils'; but give them the titles of great men."

The missionaries were taken back to their former residence, which had been fully repaired at the expense of the mandarins.

A stone tablet was placed at the entrance of the house, stating that the foreigners were there with the full recognition of the authorities.

Several days later, on November 29, 1868, Hudson and Maria's fourth son was born in that home. They named him Charles Edward.

To the missionaries it looked like the unsettling Yangchow events could now be put behind them. They had no way of knowing that further difficulties arising from the Yangchow incident were about to come upon the CIM, only this time in their homeland.

Strength through the Darkest Days

When news of the Yangchow episode and its aftermath reached England there was considerable public response against both the British consular authorities and mission organizations such as the CIM. Many thought that missionaries were stirring up trouble by demanding the protection of gunboats in their misled crusade against ancient forms of Chinese worship. In an age when intercontinental communication was quite slow, it was feared that if consuls were not more careful, Britain would be thrust into another war before the government even had the opportunity to consider the matter.

For four or five months, beginning in December of 1868, this was a pressing subject in England's daily newspapers. Hudson and the activities of the CIM were very much at the focal point of the controversy. Much inaccurate information was disseminated to the public.

William Berger, the CIM's head representative in England, had to shoulder the bulk of the responsibility in properly responding to those developments. On December 17 he wrote Hudson:

> The excitement, indeed I may almost say storm, seems bursting over us now. The *Times* is very severe, and incorrect in some things. Whether to reply to the false statements I scarcely know. At present the Yangchow outrage is the all-absorbing subject. Our letters today, I think, number from twenty to thirty.

In March of 1869 the British House of Lords debated the issue of missionary activity in China. Some argued that Britain had no right to send Christian missionaries to the inland of China and that they all ought to be recalled. Those of a more moderate viewpoint suggested that missionaries should follow British trade rather than seeking to open up new locations themselves. Still others spoke persuasively in favor of continued support for unrestricted missionary activity throughout China.

In the end Britain placed no restrictions on the activities of its Christian missionaries in China. However, the CIM was hurt through the negative publicity it received during this affair. Contributions to the organization fell off sharply and, for the first time in their two and a half years in China, CIM missionaries on the field faced a severe shortage of funds.

That spring and summer Hudson passed through a marked spiritual crisis over what he perceived to be a lack of consistent holiness in his life. For several months he had been reading a series of articles on holiness written by R. Pearsall Smith in the *Revival* magazine. These articles emphasized "the deeper spiritual life" or "the exchanged life" whereby believers could supposedly experience unbroken "union with Christ" and habitual victory over sin. Hudson became deeply troubled because, despite his most noble desires and diligent efforts, he continued to sin and did not always live in close communion with the Lord.

On October 17, 1869, after he had worked through that period of deep personal struggle, he wrote retrospectively of it in a letter to his sister Amelia (now Mrs. Benjamin Broomhall):

My mind has been greatly exercised for six or eight months past, feeling the need personally, and for our Mission, of more holiness, life, power in our souls. But personal need stood first and was the greatest. I felt the ingratitude, the danger, the sin of not living nearer to God. I prayed, agonized, fasted, strove, made resolutions, read the Word more diligently, sought more time for retirement and meditation—but all was without effect.

Every day, almost every hour, the consciousness of sin oppressed me. I knew that if I could only abide in Christ all would be well, but I *could not*. I began the day with prayer, determined not to take my eye from Him for a moment; but pressure of duties, sometimes very trying, constant inter-ruptions apt to be so wearing, often caused me to forget Him. Then one's nerves get so fretted in this climate that temptations to irritability, hard thoughts, and sometimes unkind words are all the more difficult to control. Each day brought its register of sin and failure, of lack of power. To will was indeed present with me, but how to perform I found not.

Then came the question, "Is there *no* rescue? Must it be thus to the end—constant conflict and, instead of victory, too often defeat?" How, too, could I preach with sincerity that to those who receive Jesus, "to them gave He power to become the sons of God" (*i.e.*, God-like) when it was not so in my own experience? Instead of growing stronger, I seemed to be getting weaker and to have less power against sin; and no wonder, for faith and even hope were getting very low. I felt I *was* a child of God: His Spirit in my heart would cry, in spite of all, "Abba, Father." But to rise to my privileges as a child, I was utterly powerless.

For Hudson the breakthrough came on Saturday, September 4. Working in Chinkiang at the time, he received a letter from John McCarthy with whom he had previously discussed the topic of pursuing holiness. Among other things, McCarthy wrote:

Do you know, dear brother, I now think that this striving, effort, longing, hoping for better days to come, is not the true way to happiness, holiness or usefulness. To *let* my loving Savior work in me *His will*, my sanctification, is what I would live for by His grace. Abiding, not striving nor struggling; looking off unto Him; trusting Him for present power; trusting Him to subdue all inward corruption; resting in the love of an almighty Savior, in the conscious joy of a *complete* salvation, a salvation "from all sin" (this is *His* Word); willing that His will should truly be supreme.

How then to have our faith increased? Only by thinking of all that Jesus *is*, and all He is *for us*: His life, His death, His work, He Himself as revealed to us in the Word, to be the subject of our constant thoughts. Not a striving to have faith, or to increase our faith, but a looking off to the Faithful One seems all we need.

Hudson's attention was especially arrested by that final remark of McCarthy. As he later related to Amelia:

When my agony of soul was at its height, a sentence in a letter from dear McCarthy was used to remove the scales from my eyes, and the Spirit of God revealed the truth of *our oneness* with *Jesus* as I had never known it before. As I read I saw it all! "If we believe *not*, He abideth faithful." I looked to Jesus and saw that He had said, "*I* will never leave *you*."

"Ah, *there* is rest!" I thought. "I have striven in vain to rest in Him. I'll strive no more. For has *He* not promised to abide with me—never to leave me, never to fail me?"

A few days after reading McCarthy's letter, Hudson went to Yangchow and spent the night in the home of Mr. and Mrs. Charles Judd, a CIM couple who had served in China for about a year. Hudson was so joyously preoccupied with his recent spiritual breakthrough that he failed to extend a proper greeting when Charles welcomed him into their home. Instead, pacing back and forth across the room with his hands clasped behind his back, he exclaimed: "Oh, Mr. Judd, God has made me a new man! God has made me a new man!"

As they visited late into the evening, Hudson shared further: "I have not got to *make* myself a branch. The Lord Jesus tells me I *am* a branch. I am *part of Him*, and have just to believe it and act upon it. If I go to the bank in Shanghai, having an account, and ask for fifty dollars, the clerk cannot refuse it to my outstretched hand and say that it belongs to Mr. Taylor. What belongs to Mr. Taylor my hand may take. It is a member of my body. And I am a member of Christ, and may take all I need of His fullness. I have seen it long enough in the Bible, but I *believe* it now as a living reality."

That change of perspective proved significant for Hudson throughout the remainder of his life. Charles Judd was just one of many CIM associates who bore testimony of the transformation they witnessed in the head of their mission after that:

> He was a joyous man now, a bright, happy Christian. He had been a toiling, burdened one before, with latterly not much rest of soul. It was resting in Jesus now, and letting Him do the work—which makes all the difference!
>
> Whenever he spoke in meetings, after that, a new power seemed to flow from him, and in the practical things of life a new peace possessed him. Troubles did not worry him as before. He cast everything on God in a new way, and gave more time to prayer. Instead of working late at night, he began to go to bed earlier, rising at five in the morning to give two hours before the work of the day began to Bible study and prayer. Thus his own soul was fed, and from him flowed the living water to others.

Because of criticisms of the CIM that surfaced over the Yangchow affair, giving to the mission during May through September of 1869 was down more than one thousand pounds compared with the same five-month period in the previous year.

To make matters worse, in November serious difficulties erupted at the CIM's newly opened station at its farthest point inland, Anking. At first it was rumored that the missionaries there had been killed in the riot, but that report proved false. Missionaries were later able to return to Anking and establish a vibrant work there.

God used a prominent Christian in England to bring marked encouragement to the hearts of CIM missionaries as that challenging year drew to a close. George Muller was well known among Christians for his ministry to thousands of orphans in Bristol. He also was an active promoter and supporter of various foreign missionary causes.

On December 31, 1869, Hudson received letters from William Berger and George Muller. Berger's stated:

> Mr. Muller, after due consideration, has requested the names of *all* the brethren and sisters connected with the CIM, as he thinks it well to send help as he is able to each one, unless we know of anything to hinder. Surely the Lord knew our funds were sinking, and thus put it into the heart of His honored servant to help.

Muller's correspondence included individual checks written to the missionary couples and single missionaries serving under the CIM at the time. He explained in his letter to all the missionaries:

> My chief object, is to tell you that I love you in the Lord, that I feel deeply interested about the Lord's work in China, and that I pray daily for you. I thought it might be a little encouragement to you in your difficulties, trials, hardships and disappointments to hear of one more who felt for you and who remembered you before the Lord.

Muller helped support all thirty-three missionaries on the CIM staff that year. Throughout the several years that followed he contributed nearly two thousand pounds (equaling ten thousand dollars) annually to the CIM.

Early in 1870 Hudson and Maria decided that their four oldest children should be sent back to England to safeguard their health from the many threatening diseases to which they were regularly exposed in China. Emily Blatchley, who was especially close to the children and who was herself battling tuberculosis, volunteered to escort the children to their homeland. Only Charles, still just a toddler, would stay with his parents.

In February, however, just as the family was setting out from Yangchow to Shanghai, five-year-old Samuel suddenly became gravely ill. For nearly a year he had suffered from enteritis. Within hours he died, and the family crossed the Yangtze to bury his body in the mission's small cemetery at Chinkiang. After that the group continued on to Shanghai from which, three or four weeks later, Emily and the three oldest Taylor children sailed to England.

The following summer another menacing wave of strong anti-foreign sentiment swept across China. In the coastal city of Tientsin, far to the north, a group of Roman Catholic priests and nuns and even the French consul were brutally murdered. Unrest developed in nearly every city where CIM associates ministered. Women missionaries and their children needed to be removed from several of those towns. A number of them came to stay with the Taylors in Chinkiang. For a time it looked like all the CIM stations along the Yangtze might have to be temporarily abandoned by the men as well.

In the midst of such stressful circumstances Maria gave birth on July 7 to a son, whom they named Noel. Maria, suffering from cholera and internal bleeding, grew steadily weaker in the days that followed the delivery. At first Noel seemed to be doing well, but then he developed a severe mouth infection and diarrhea. The infant died on July 20 after having lived only thirteen days. Maria was not well enough to attend the funeral, but she did choose two hymns to be used at the service.

The funeral was held on Friday evening, July 22. Later that same evening Hudson was visiting quietly with a missionary couple in the room that adjoined Maria's bedroom when he heard her faintly call his name. Rushing to her, he found her standing beside her bed, unable to speak or move. He lifted her back into bed and sought to make her as comfortable as possible. Her heart had begun to palpitate rapidly. He gave her some food and medicine, and she drifted off to sleep. As a lady missionary stayed by Maria's bedside, Hudson and a trio of other missionaries gathered in the next room to pray for her.

When the sun rose the next morning, Hudson could clearly see that Maria was dying. That realization came as a stunning blow to him. Up until the previous evening it had not occurred to any of them that her earthly sojourn, too, might be nearing its end. She was only thirty-three years old.

Hot tears welled up in Hudson's eyes and spilled down his cheeks. When he had composed himself, he quietly asked her, "My darling, do you know that you are dying?"

"Dying!" she responded with surprise. "Do you think so? What makes you think so?"

"I can see it, darling. Your strength is giving way."

"Can it be so? I feel no pain, only weariness."

"Yes, you are going Home. You will soon be with Jesus."

"I am so sorry," she breathed softly, then paused as if correcting herself for feeling that way.

"You are not sorry to go to be with Jesus?" he queried gently.

A look of complete peace and joy came to her face as she answered: "Oh, no! It is not that. You know, darling, that for ten years past there has not been a cloud between me and my Savior. I cannot be sorry to go to Him. But it does grieve me to leave you alone at such a time. Yet He will be with you and meet all your need."

A number of missionaries and Chinese Christians gathered around her bed to say farewell. She shared a final message that she desired to be passed on to her children. After that, her strength all but gone, she put one arm around Hudson's neck, placed her other hand on his head and offered a final prayer of blessing on him. Her lips moved, but no sound came from her mouth. Then she slipped into a peaceful sleep.

As her breathing became lighter and lighter, Hudson knelt beside her bed and prayed: "Dear Lord, I now commit Maria to You. Thank You for giving her to me, and for these twelve and a half years of happiness which we have had together. Thank You, too, for taking her now to Your own blessed presence. My Master, this day I solemnly dedicate myself anew to Your service." At nine o'clock that morning Maria quietly stepped into eternity.

A few days later Hudson wrote William Berger:

And now, dear brother, what shall I say of the Lord's dealings with me and mine? I know not! My heart is overwhelmed with gratitude and praise. My eyes flow with tears of mingled joy and sorrow. When I think of my loss, my heart—nigh to breaking—rises in thankfulness to Him Who has spared *her* such sorrow and made her so unspeakably happy. My tears are more tears of joy than of grief.

But most of all I joy in God through our Lord Jesus Christ—in His works, His ways, His providence, in Himself. He is giving me to prove (to know by trial) "what is that good and acceptable and perfect will of God." I do rejoice in that will. It is acceptable to me; it is perfect; it is love in action.

To his mother he wrote on August 4:

From my inmost soul I delight in the knowledge that God does or deliberately permits *all* things, and causes all things to work together for good to those who love Him. *He* and He only knew what my dear wife was to me. He knew how the light of my eyes and the joy of my heart were in her.

But He saw that it was good to take her. Good indeed for her, and in His love He took her painlessly. And not less good for me who must henceforth toil and suffer alone—yet not alone, for God is nearer to me than ever. And now I have to tell *Him* all my sorrows and difficulties, as I used to tell dear Maria. And as she cannot join me in intercession, to rest in the knowledge of Jesus' intercession; to walk a little less by feeling, a little less by sight, a little more by faith.

18

The Growth of
the Mission

The months that followed Maria's death were, naturally, extremely difficult ones for Hudson. He was terribly lonely without the companionship of her and their children. For several weeks he suffered from spells of insomnia. Despite his personal difficulties, he continued to actively carry out his responsibilities as head of the CIM, advising missionaries at various stations and tending to numerous administrative concerns.

In the summer of 1871, one year after Maria's death, he sailed back to England to spend some time with his children and to visit supporters. He was accompanied by his two-year-old son, Charlie, as well as missionaries James and Elizabeth Meadows and Jennie Faulding.

Hudson and Jennie spent considerable time together during the voyage. During her five years of service in Hangchow, Jennie had been used of God to win more than fifty Chinese adults to Christ and had established a number of schools for children.

As they visited throughout the voyage, Hudson and Jennie discovered that they were coming to have a romantic affection for each other.

Before the journey was completed they had decided to marry. The wedding took place in London on November 28, 1871. Hudson was thirty-nine years old and Jennie was twenty-eight. The following January, Hudson, Jennie, and the children moved to No. 6 Pyrland Road in the district of Newington Green on the northern outskirts of London.

Because of declining health, William Berger wished to resign as the supervisor of CIM affairs in England. Emily Blatchley agreed to assume many of the responsibilities he had borne. In addition, the Council of Management of the CIM, later called simply the London Council, was formed to help oversee those concerns.

Leaving the children under Emily's care, Hudson and Jennie returned to China, arriving there in October of 1872. They found conditions at some of the CIM stations at a low ebb, with missionaries discouraged and Chinese Christians backslidden. Hudson, often accompanied by Jennie, proceeded to tour all the stations, seeking to encourage and strengthen missionaries and Chinese Christian workers alike. "Things will soon look *up*, with God's blessing, if looked after," he confidently expressed to her. The Lord used their conscientious, prayerful efforts to restore sound spiritual health to the mission's work.

The CIM continued to be challenged by a tightness of funds during that period, but Hudson's faith never wavered. In April 1874 he told Jennie, "The balance in hand yesterday was sixty-seven cents! The Lord reigns: herein is our joy and confidence." To another missionary he stated, when the balance had sunk even lower, "We have twenty-five cents and all the promises of God!"

That June, Hudson had a nasty fall from a ladder in which he landed heavily on his heels, resulting in a sprained ankle and some compressed vertebrae. The seriousness of the injury to his spine did not become readily apparent until several weeks later.

In August he and Jennie sailed for England, having received reports that Emily Blatchley's health was failing because of her tuberculosis. They needed to make other arrangements for the care of their children as well as attend to pressing missions matters at home. Upon their arrival, they were stunned and saddened to learn that Emily had died while they were at sea.

Hudson's own physical condition continued to deteriorate until, shortly after their arrival in London late in 1874, his lower limbs were virtually paralyzed. The doctor placed him on strict bed rest. For a time it appeared unlikely that they would ever be able to return to China.

Despite that fact, from his bed in the house on Pyrland Road in January of 1875 the indomitable Hudson dictated an article titled "An Appeal for Prayer on behalf of more than a hundred and fifty millions of Chinese." In it he asked Christians to pray earnestly that eighteen pioneer evangelists would be raised up that year to carry the gospel to the nine inland provinces of China that were still unevangelized.

The article was printed in several Christian publications. As a result, over sixty individuals made inquiry that year about becoming pioneer evangelists. The Taylors' home was wholly inadequate to handle the number of candidates who came for screening. The mission was able to lease the adjacent houses at Nos. 2 and 4 Pyrland Road in order to meet its expanding need for housing and office space.

Jennie had recently received a large legacy of over four thousand pounds from a wealthy uncle. She donated the entire sum to help subsidize the cost of sending and supporting the eighteen evangelists as soon as they were available.

That spring Hudson also launched, in place of the CIM's *Occasional Paper*, an illustrated monthly periodical which came to be called *China's Millions*. The new publication was quite an innovation in its day and greatly helped to promote interest in the mission's endeavors.

Hudson experienced a gradual healing from his paralysis. After two months in bed he was able to sit up in a chair for a couple hours each day. After three more months he could get up and down stairs by himself. He at first walked with the aid of a cane but eventually was able to get around without it.

By February of 1876 twenty men, including six CIM veteran missionaries, had been accepted to go as God's answer to the request for eighteen inland evangelists. Six women also went to China that year under the auspices of the CIM. Hudson himself, accompanied by a party of eight new missionaries, was able to return to China that September. This time Jennie stayed in London to care for the children, including the son, Ernest, and daughter, Amy, to whom she had given birth during the past eighteen months.

On September 14, 1876, the Chefoo Convention was signed, giving foreigners with a passport the right to travel safely throughout China. Within four months CIM missionaries penetrated six new inland provinces, traveling to parts of China never before seen by foreigners. Their arrival was greeted with a mixture of friendliness and hostility.

Hudson soon found himself under a mountain of administrative responsibilities. Frequently he would relax at the end of a long day of pressures and concerns by sitting down at a small reed organ to play and sing some of his favorite hymns. Nearly always he included: "Jesus, I am resting, resting, in the joy of what Thou art; I am finding out the greatness of Thy loving heart."

One day missionary George Nichol was with him in his office when a number of letters arrived that brought news of serious rioting in two of the CIM stations. Thinking that the mission head might want to be left alone to ponder and pray about those weighty matters, Nichol was turning to leave when suddenly he heard Hudson begin to whistle softly that familiar refrain, "Jesus, I Am Resting, Resting."

Surprised, the young missionary turned back and exclaimed, "How *can* you whistle, when our friends are in so much danger?"

"Would you have me to be anxious and troubled?" Hudson responded calmly. "That would not help them, and would certainly incapacitate me for my work. I have just to roll the burden on the Lord."

Hudson returned to England late in 1877, just in time to celebrate a joyous Christmas season with Jennie and the children. At that time the northern provinces of China were experiencing widespread famine because of a prolonged drought and repeated crop failures. Some six million people were seriously threatened with starvation. The CIM authorized its missionaries in those famine regions to take in two hundred orphans.

Being unable to return to China at that time himself, Hudson asked Jennie to go in his stead to supervise the establishment of the orphan ministry. After Jennie prayerfully concluded that the Lord would have her to do so, Hudson's sister, Amelia, who by then had ten children of her own, stated, "If Jennie is called to China, I am called to care for her children."

In April of 1878 Jennie sailed for China with seven young men and women. That year nearly thirty new missionaries went out under the CIM.

The following spring, 1879, Hudson was able to join Jennie in China. The next two years were largely devoted to helping CIM missionaries establish new bases in previously unreached inland regions. Jennie returned to England to tend to family matters after her mother and both of Hudson's parents died during the summer of 1881.

That November Hudson met with a small group of missionaries at the CIM station in Wuchang, 425 miles west of Shanghai, to discuss the need for further expansion. One afternoon as Hudson and missionary A. G. Parrott were walking and discussing the situation, the words of Luke 10:1—"after these things the Lord appointed other seventy also"—came distinctly to Hudson's mind. Sharing the verse with his companion, Hudson wondered aloud, "Could this impression be of the Lord?"

Initially it seemed like too much to ask for seventy new missionaries, especially in light of the fact that giving to the mission had been down that year. But as they continued to walk, Parrott's foot struck against something in the grass. "See what I have found!" he exclaimed, stooping over to pick up a string of one hundred Chinese cash. "If we have to come to the hills for it, God is well able to give us all the money needed!"

The two returned to their associates to discuss and pray about that possibility. As they did, all reached the settled conviction that God would have them to ask for seventy more missionaries. They agreed to pray daily that the seventy would be raised up and sent out in the next three years.

"If only we could meet again and have a united praise meeting when the last of the seventy has reached China!" enthused one of the missionaries.

"We shall be widely scattered by then," remarked another. "But why not have the praise meeting now? Why not give thanks for the seventy before we separate?"

That suggestion met with the approval of all and resulted in a faith-filled prayer meeting of praise and thanksgiving. In January 1882 Hudson drafted and seventy-seven members of the mission signed an appeal to the home churches, asking them to prayerfully support the raising up of the seventy. The response started slowly, with only eleven new CIM missionaries being sent out that first year.

Hudson returned to England in the spring of 1883, nearly a year and a half since he had last been with Jennie. By now the CIM was well thought of throughout the British Isles and Hudson Taylor's had become something of a household name. Letters of support poured in from everywhere. During a ten-month period in 1883–84 Hudson personally responded to more than twenty-six hundred letters. "If you are not dead yet," one child wrote him, "I want to send you the money I have saved up to help the little boys and girls of China to love Jesus."

Invitations to speak were also prolific. Charles Spurgeon invited Hudson to preach at the London Metropolitan Tabernacle. Taylor also spoke with great power and influence at a conference in Salisbury. At the conference's closing praise meeting, despite the fact that the CIM was never mentioned and no offering was taken, some people consecrated their lives to service in China while others emptied their purses and even took off their gold watches, rings, and other jewelry to give for the cause of missions.

Twenty new CIM missionaries left for China in 1883 followed by forty-six more in 1884. The prayers for the seventy actually yielded seventy-seven.

Hudson ventured back to China in January of 1885. The next month saw the departure of the highly celebrated "Cambridge Seven." That group was made up of young men from privileged homes who, after distinguishing themselves at the university, gave up opportunities to gain further worldly fame and fortune in order to heed Christ's higher call to missionary service. As they shared their inspiring personal testimonies at a series of huge public rallies in England and Scotland before leaving for China, many were won to faith in Jesus, Christians were challenged to serve the Lord with greater commitment, and the CIM came to be held in even higher regard.

That year Hudson began initiating some changes in how the CIM's work was superintended on the field. As the mission's ministry had grown over the years, it had become increasingly difficult for him to properly supervise the entire work all on his own. He desired to establish a China Council, made up of district superintendents, which would assist him in carrying out the administrative oversight of the mission. Some of the first regional superintendents were appointed in 1885 and John Stevenson was named Hudson's deputy director.

During the summer of 1886 Hudson traveled for the first time into the northern inland province of Shansi, meeting with missionaries and Chinese Christians in various places to encourage them in their ministry efforts. At the close of the Shansi itineration, he set out with Montagu Beauchamp, one of the Cambridge Seven, on a memorable twenty-four-day overland journey to the city of Hanchung near the border of Szechwan Province. The CIM desired to establish a work in that province by year's end.

Because of the intense heat, they sometimes traveled at night. They had two mules, and Hudson rode one, but the muscular Beauchamp, a former oarsman for the Cambridge rowing team, preferred to walk. The younger missionary, who had difficulty sleeping during the daytime, later reported: "Walking at night, I have been so sleepy that even the motion could not keep me awake, and have fallen right down while plodding on—the tumble rousing one for the time being!"

It was the rainy season so their clothing repeatedly got soaked clear through. They also had to contend with crossing swollen rivers and streams. Several times Beauchamp waded waist deep across fast-moving streams with Hudson on his shoulders and a Chinese man hanging on either side to weigh them down and help give them stability!

One evening they were detained at a small village by a driving rain. As the village had no inn, the only shelter they could find was a pigsty. So they turned out the hog, borrowed some benches, took the doors off their hinges to use as beds, and wrapped up in their wool blankets to try to get a little sleep. The pig returned shortly, broke through the makeshift door they had set up, then contentedly settled down to spend the night with them!

Food was sometimes quite difficult to come by during the journey. Early one morning, when they were very hungry, Beauchamp heard Hudson singing and caught the words, "We thank Thee, Lord, for this our food."

"But, Mr. Taylor," he could not help but inquire, "where is the food?"

"It cannot be far away," Hudson responded cheerfully. "Our Father knows we are hungry and will send our breakfast soon." Then he added with a twinkle in his eye, "But *you* will have to wait and say your grace when it comes, while *I* shall be ready to begin at once!"

And so it turned out. Just minutes later they encountered a man who was selling ready-cooked rice and were able to buy themselves a satisfying meal.

Beauchamp also observed during that journey the private discipline that Hudson maintained in order to nourish his spiritual life and health. He afterward divulged of the mission director:

> He would invariably get his quiet time an hour before dawn, and then possibly sleep again. When I woke to feed the animals I always found him reading the Bible by the light of his candle. No matter what the surroundings or the noise in those dirty inns, he never neglected this. He used to pray on such journeys lying down, for he usually spent long times in prayer, and to kneel would have been too exhausting.

Upon reaching Hanchung, Hudson was delighted to see the medical work and school that were being run by CIM missionaries. Discussions were devoted to penetrating Szechwan with the gospel, and a day of prayer and fasting was spent seeking the Lord's guidance and blessing in that potential undertaking. Before the end of the year the first CIM missionaries had begun laboring in that province.

In November of 1886 the China Council gathered for the first time, meeting at Anking more than three hundred miles up the Yangtze River from Shanghai. Sensing the crucial importance of those meetings for the future direction and welfare of the mission, the entire first week was devoted to prayer and fasting.

A couple of months earlier, Deputy Director John Stevenson had suggested that the mission start earnestly praying for one hundred new missionaries to be sent out to China during the following year, 1887. At first some of the China Council members were inclined to think that Stevenson's proposal was too ambitious. But before the Anking meetings were concluded, Hudson, Stevenson, and the entire council became convinced that such a request was in keeping with God's will and started praying it in faith.

Hudson and Stevenson spent a few days tending to some administrative matters after the council adjourned. Stevenson was with Hudson one day as the latter paced back and forth across a room while dictating letters to his secretary. When he stated, "We are praying for and expecting a hundred new missionaries to come out in 1887," the secretary looked up with an incredulous smile.

Both Hudson and Stevenson saw the younger man's disbelieving look. Immediately Hudson stated with deep conviction, "If you showed me a photograph of the whole hundred, taken in China, I could not be more sure than I am now."

He and his missionary associates began to sing a little prayer at each meal:

Oh send the hundred workers, Lord,
    Those of Thy heart and mind and choice,
To tell Thy love both far and wide—
    So shall we praise Thee and rejoice:
And above the rest this note shall swell,
    My Jesus hath done all things well.

An elderly veteran missionary in Shanghai commented to Hudson: "I am delighted to hear that you are praying for large reinforcements. You will not get a hundred, of course, within the year; but you will get many more than if you did not ask for them."

Hudson responded: "Thank you for your interest. We have the joy of knowing our prayers are answered now. And I feel sure that, if spared, you will share that joy by welcoming the last of the hundred to China!"

On February 18, 1887, Hudson arrived back in London. Throughout the remainder of the year he maintained a Herculean schedule: speaking at churches and conferences in most large towns and cities throughout the British Isles; writing an average of more than a dozen letters a day; interviewing hundreds of potential candidates who responded to the appeal for one hundred new missionaries. In addition, he conferred extensively with the London Council and John Stevenson about administrative issues that needed to be addressed in both England and China.

During the year an astounding total of six hundred men and women volunteered for service in China. The London Council maintained its high standards with regard to qualified candidates, selecting only one in six for service with the CIM. By year's end, 102 new missionaries had sailed for China. As Hudson had predicted, the elderly missionary who doubted that the full number requested would be supplied was there in Shanghai to greet the last of the one hundred.

19

Trusting to the End

L ate in 1887, Henry Frost of Attica, New York, first corresponded with, then visited Hudson in England about
the possibility of establishing a North American branch
of the CIM. Hudson was not at first receptive to the proposal,
believing that a British missionary organization would not be
readily accepted in America.

Knowing that Taylor was thinking of returning to China the
following year, Frost queried, "Would you be willing to travel to
China by way of America, if you were invited to speak at Niagara
on the Lake and at Mr. Moody's conference at Northfield?"

"Yes, I think such invitations might be accepted," responded
Hudson.

The next summer, 1888, Hudson visited America for the first
time. He spoke at the large Niagara Conference, then traveled
on to Chicago to minister at the invitation of Dwight Moody, the
famous American evangelist. After Hudson left Niagara on the
Lake, an offering of nearly two thousand dollars was received
and entrusted to Frost along with the request, "Please pass this

to Mr. Taylor and suggest that it should be used for American workers in connection with the CIM."

Gradually and prayerfully Hudson became convinced that such a proposal was in keeping with God's will. He began making strong appeals for Americans to go to China.

While traveling by train to Montreal with the CIM director, Frost read a disparaging magazine article titled "Hudson Taylor in Toronto." The article upset Frost and, desiring to shield Taylor from it, he attempted to hide it under a stack of papers. Hudson, however, had noticed the article and retrieved it to read:

> Hudson Taylor is rather disappointing. I had in my mind an idea of what great missionaries should look like. He being professedly one of the great missionaries of modern times must be such as they. But he is not. A stranger would never notice him on the street, except perhaps to say that he is a good-natured looking Englishman. Nor is his voice in the least degree majestic. He displays little oratorical power. He elicits little applause, launches no thunderbolts. Even our [Jonathan] Goforth used to plead more eloquently for China's millions, and apparently with more effect. It is quite possible that were Mr. Taylor, under another name, to preach as a candidate in our Ontario vacancies there are those who would begrudge him his probationer's pay.

After finishing the article Hudson sat quietly for several minutes. Then, smiling, he said to Frost: "This is very just criticism, for it is all true. I have often thought that God made me little in order that He might show what a great God He is."

By mid-September more than forty Americans had applied to join the CIM. Eight women and six men were approved. They accompanied Hudson across the Rocky Mountains on the Canadian Pacific Railway and, in October, sailed west from Vancouver for Shanghai.

One year later, in November and December of 1889, Hudson visited Sweden and Denmark, having been invited to go there in an effort to develop closer ties between Scandinavian mission societies and the CIM. Everywhere he went he spoke to large, attentive audiences which gave generously to support missions work in China. Queen Sophia even requested a private audience with him at the palace five miles outside Stockholm.

In the spring of 1890 he had the opportunity to deliver the opening address at the interdenominational General Missionary Conference in Shanghai. He challenged all the mission societies ministering in China to collectively seek to raise up an additional one thousand evangelists in order to help fulfill, more literally, Christ's command to take the gospel to every creature. The conference adopted a tempered form of his proposal, issuing an appeal for a thousand men to come within the next five years to carry out all forms of missionary endeavor including teaching and medical work. As it turned out, 1,153 new missionaries (673 women and 480 men) did go to China in response to that joint appeal.

That August 1890 he ventured to Australia where a number of Christians were eagerly desiring to learn more about how they could play a part in the evangelization of China. Again he ministered to attentive audiences at numerous meetings. At a large Presbyterian church in Melbourne the man introducing Hudson went on and on about his considerable accomplishments before ending with a flourish by presenting him as "our illustrious guest."

Hudson stepped to the podium and stood in silence for a moment. Then he stated quietly, "Dear friends, I am the little servant of an illustrious Master."

At the end of November he sailed back to China, this time with the first party of CIM missionaries from Australia and Tasmania—four men and eight women. In Shanghai a special Christmas treat awaited him: Jennie had been able to return to China for the first time in nine years. She and Hudson would never again have to endure a long separation as they had on several occasions throughout the past decade.

During the first four months of 1891 seven parties comprising a total of seventy-eight new CIM missionaries arrived in China from Europe, North America, and Australia. In addition, fifty missionaries from Scandinavia arrived in two groups that February. They came to serve with the Scandinavian Alliance Mission, which intended to partner as an associate mission with the CIM in carrying the gospel to inland China.

With such rapid growth, it was nearly inevitable that the CIM experienced some marked growing pains in the early 1890s. A deep difference of opinion developed over whether the China Council or the London Council should have executive powers over the mission. Hudson and the China Council insisted that a fundamental principle upon which the mission had been founded was that its China affairs would be directed from China. They also suggested that, given the increasingly international makeup of the CIM, it was important for the mission to be directed by an executive committee that did not appear to favor British interests.

The London Council, on the other hand, argued that it bore the responsibility of answering to the mission's supporters and, therefore, ought to be given greater authority. In addition, some CIM missionaries complained to the London Council about policy and procedure decisions that the China Council had already passed. Nearly thirty missionaries ended up resigning from the CIM. Giving to the mission dropped noticeably as word got out about these tensions within the organization.

As 1892 wore on, special times of prayer and fasting were devoted to seeking the Lord's solution in working through the crisis. Hudson returned to England where he was able to iron out some of the difficulties with the London Council members. Early in 1893 Henry Frost visited London and helped promote further resolution. The controversy was settled when it was decided that the CIM's China, London, and North American Councils would not have executive power but would meet to advise directors who oversaw the mission's work in various locations.

Hudson and Jennie shared two more terms of active service in China—April 1894 to May 1896 and January 1898 to September 1899. During both those terms political conditions in the country were unstable and anti-foreign sentiment was pronounced. In 1895 China lost a war with Japan over the right to control Korea. After that, European nations began pressuring a weakened China for increased influence and opportunities that threatened to make it more subject to the West.

Some of China's political and educational leaders believed it was time to adopt Western ways, and introduced reforms that pointed in that direction. Others, intent on safeguarding traditional Chinese values and autonomy, desired to see all foreigners driven from the country. In September of 1898 the dowager empress took charge of the government and executed many of the reformers. Local riots became commonplace.

Since most Westerners in the inland provinces were missionaries, hostilities against foreigners were commonly directed against them. November of that same year brought the ominous news of the martyrdom of two CIM workers, Australian missionary William Fleming and his Chinese assistant Pan Shoushan, in the southwestern province of Kweichow.

From the fall of 1899 through the spring of 1900 Hudson carried out a number of speaking engagements in Australia,

New Zealand, and the United States. That April he addressed thirty-five hundred people from over one hundred mission societies at the Ecumenical Missionary Conference held in New York's Carnegie Hall.

The next month he traveled to Boston to speak at a series of meetings with the popular American Bible teacher and author, A. T. Pierson. There Hudson suffered a partial mental breakdown. Speaking at a meeting, he seemed to lose his train of thought, then began repeating the same two sentences over and over again: "You may trust the Lord too little, but you can never trust Him too much. 'If we believe not, yet He abideth faithful; He cannot deny Himself.'"

Pierson, who quickly stepped forward to take over the meeting for Hudson, later reflected:

> There was something pathetic and poetic in the very fact that this repetition was the first visible sign of his breakdown. For was it not this very sentiment and this very quotation that he had kept repeating to himself and to all his fellow workers during all the years of his missionary work? A blessed sentence to break down upon, which had been the buttress of his whole life of consecrated endeavor.

Cutting short their visit to America, Hudson and Jennie returned to London in June. He was too ill to speak at meetings or even write letters. They then traveled to Davos, Switzerland, so he could convalesce there.

In China, meanwhile, local militia units had been training for several months to defend the country against further foreign encroachments. These units, which became known as "Boxers" because they practiced gymnastic exercises, adopted the slogan "Destroy the foreigner." In June 1900 the dowager empress did the unthinkable by issuing an edict ordering foreigners to be killed throughout the empire.

The Boxer rebellion was as much an anti-foreign as anti-Christian movement. However, missionaries and Chinese Christians bore the brunt of the uprising. In the Beijing area upwards to twenty thousand Roman Catholics were massacred, and in Shansi Province another two thousand Catholic Christians lost their lives. Fewer Protestant nationals were killed in the uprising, but more Protestant than Catholic missionaries were martyred. Over 130 Protestant missionaries and 50 of their children perished. The CIM suffered worse casualties than any other society with 58 missionaries and 21 missionary children being killed.

Some effort was made to shield Hudson, who was still in a state of physical and mental exhaustion, from a full knowledge of what had happened as news of the Boxer massacres reached Davos through a series of telegrams from China. As he became aware of the tragic developments, he stated: "I cannot read; I cannot think; I cannot even pray; but I can trust."

In July, Jennie wrote to the suffering members of their beloved missionary family: "Day and night our thoughts are with you all. My dear husband says, 'I would do all I could to help them. And our heavenly Father, who has the power, *will* do for each one according to His wisdom and love.'"

After Hudson gradually regained his health, he and Jennie went back to England for a few months. Just before his seventieth birthday, in May of 1902, they returned to Switzerland, settling in the little village of Chevalleyres on the northern edge of Lake Geneva. There they enjoyed taking rail and steamer excursions together. Hudson spent many hours studying flowers and the stars, and revived his long-neglected hobby of photography. Although he had been able to concentrate only on "easy reading" since his breakdown, in 1902 he did succeed in reading through the Bible for the fortieth time in forty years.

It was discovered in July of 1903 that Jennie had a cancerous tumor. The cancer was so far advanced that an operation was considered useless. Her strength slowly declined until in June of the following year she was no longer able to dress herself. Hudson's son, Howard, himself a medical doctor and CIM missionary, came to assist Jennie as did her daughter, Amy.

To Howard's wife, Geraldine, Jennie wrote: "You'll know the comfort that dear Howard is, and Amy and dear father—all so loving and ready to spoil me in everything. So tenderly the Lord is dealing with us! There seems nothing to wish for, only to praise."

The evening of July 29 she found it difficult to breathe. "No pain, no pain," she kept saying reassuringly to Hudson who was at her bedside. Before dawn the next morning she whispered to him, "Ask Him to take me quickly."

He hesitated, then prayed simply, "Dear Father, free her waiting spirit." Within five minutes the request was granted. She was sixty years old at the time of her death.

In the spring of 1905 Hudson ventured to China for the eleventh and final time. Accompanied by Howard and Geraldine, he traveled by steamboat to Changsha, the capital of Hunan, a city he had never before visited. Hunan, traditionally China's most anti-foreign province, just eight or nine years earlier had not contained a single Protestant missionary. By 1905, however, more than a hundred missionaries from thirteen societies labored there in partnership with Chinese believers.

On Saturday, June 3, a reception was held for Hudson at Changsha's CIM mission house. Missionaries from six societies attended the gathering. Hudson mingled with the guests for over an hour, an expression of pure joy on his face.

After the guests departed, Hudson went upstairs to rest. When Geraldine looked in on him a while later, she found him in bed. Apparently he had been reading a stack of letters. After adjusting the pillow more comfortably under his head, she sat down on the chair next to his bed and commented about the pictures in the *Missionary Review* magazine that lay open beside him. Suddenly a small gasp escaped from Hudson and Geraldine realized that he was lapsing into unconsciousness.

She ran to the door and cried, "Howard! Come quickly!" A moment after Howard arrived Hudson stopped breathing and stepped into the presence of his heavenly Master whom he had faithfully served for more than fifty years.

Chinese Christians insisted on buying his coffin and purchased the best they could find. The coffin was taken by boat along the Kiang and Yangtze Rivers to Chinkiang. At each CIM river station along the way flowers and wreaths were carried on board, so that by the time John Stevenson met the boat in Chinkiang, the coffin was hidden beneath a blanket of color.

Dixon Hoste, one of the Cambridge Seven and the man who had been appointed to serve as Hudson's successor as general director of the CIM, conducted the funeral service. Afterward, Hudson's body was buried in the Chinkiang cemetery next to the graves of Maria and four of their children. The stone that was erected over his grave read: "Sacred to the memory of the Rev. J. Hudson Taylor, the revered founder of the China Inland Mission, born May 21, 1832, died June 3, 1905. A man in Christ."

At the time of Hudson's death over eight hundred missionaries partnered with more than two thousand Chinese pastors, evangelists, and Bible women in proclaiming the gospel at a thousand CIM stations and outstations. In his lifetime 1.5 million pounds (equaling 7.5 million dollars) had been given to the mission to support the evangelization of inland China. As a result thirty thousand Chinese had become Christians through the ministry of the China Inland Mission.

For Further Reading

Hudson Taylor, J. Hudson Taylor (Minneapolis: Bethany, n.d.). Originally published under the title *A Retrospect*, this is Taylor's autobiography of the first half of his life up through the time when he founded the China Inland Mission.

Hudson Taylor's Spiritual Secret, Howard and Geraldine Taylor (Chicago: Moody, 1989). This is Dr. and Mrs. Taylor's classic shorter account of Hudson Taylor's life, ministry, and spiritual development.

Hudson Taylor in Early Years, The Growth of a Soul, Howard and Geraldine Taylor (London: China Inland Mission, 1911). Part 1 of the Taylors' comprehensive biography of Hudson Taylor, the volume traces his life from its beginning through his first extended term of service in China.

Hudson Taylor and the China Inland Mission, The Growth of a Work of God, Howard and Geraldine Taylor (London: China Inland Mission, 1918). In Part 2 of their voluminous biography on Hudson Taylor, Dr. and Mrs. Howard Taylor follow his life from his first furlough in England, when the China Inland Mission was founded, to his death in China four decades later.

J. Hudson Taylor, A Man in Christ, Roger Steer (Singapore: Overseas Missionary Fellowship, 1990). This work provides an engaging and informative account of Taylor's entire life.

"Hudson Taylor and Missions to China," *Christian History Magazine*, Issue 52 (Vol. XV, No. 4). The whole issue is dedicated to exploring not only Taylor's life and ministry but also many other facets of Protestant missionary endeavor in China throughout the past two centuries.

The Guided Tour series are biographical "tours" of the lives and thoughts of famous historical figures. These accounts encompass their lives, writings, and contributions to society and the Christian faith.

"A marvelous mixture of biography, history, theology, and anecdote."
—**Sinclair B. Ferguson**

THE GUIDED TOUR SERIES:

*Anne Bradstreet: A Guided Tour of the Life
and Thought of a Puritan Poet*

J. Gresham Machen: A Guided Tour of His Life and Thought

Jonathan Edwards: A Guided Tour of His Life and Thought

*Katherine Parr: A Guided Tour of the Life
and Thought of a Reformation Queen*

Martin Luther: A Guided Tour of His Life and Thought

Pages from Church History: A Guided Tour of Christian Classics

HISTORICAL FICTION FROM **P&R PUBLISHING**

To order books in this series,
visit www.prpbooks.com
Or call 1(800) 631-0094

The Chosen Daughters series highlights the lives of ordinary women who by God's grace accomplish extraordinary things.

"Our daughters today need to know God's unique purpose for them, and that girls and women can do great things for God!"
—**Neta Jackson**

THE CHOSEN DAUGHTERS SERIES:

Wings Like a Dove: The Courage of Queen Jeanne d'Albret
Dr. Oma: The Healing Wisdom of Countess Juliana Von Stolberg
Against the Tide: The Valor of Margaret Wilson
A Cup of Cold Water: The Compassion of Nurse Edith Cavell

Coming September 2011:
Weight of a Flame: The Passion of Olympia Morata

MORE BIOGRAPHIES FROM **P&R PUBLISHING**

To order books in this series,
visit www.prpbooks.com
Or call 1(800) 631-0094

American Reformed Biographies make available the best kind of historical writing—one that yields both knowledge and wisdom.

The titles in this series feature American Reformed leaders who were important representatives or interpreters of Reformed Christianity in the United States and who continue to be influential through writings and arguments still pertinent to theologians, pastors, and church members.

THE AMERICAN REFORMED BIOGRAPHIES:

Robert Lewis Dabney: A Southern Presbyterian Life

John Williamson Nevin: High Church Calvinist

Cornelius Van Til: Reformed Apologist and Churchman

James Petigru Boyce: A Southern Baptist Statesman

HISTORICAL FICTION FROM P&R PUBLISHING

Price: $14.99
To order, visit www.prpbooks.com
Or call 1(800) 631-0094

Step into the midst of the private war of one man determined to sell all for a convoluted allegiance, even at the cost of his own soul.

Told from the perspective of a sworn lifelong enemy of John Calvin, this fast-paced biographical novel is a tale of envy that escalates to violent intrigue and shameless betrayal.

"Anything Doug Bond writes is, almost now by definition, a fascinating read. But to have his skills attached to the life of John Calvin is a double treat."
—Joel Belz

"An exciting read, almost effortlessly and implicitly undoing caricatures about Calvin along the way . . . Calvin and his times brought to life in a page-turner!"
—Joel R. Beeke